True Tales™
of
Shifting Ground

Henry Billings

Melissa Stone Billings

STECK-VAUGHN
ELEMENTARY · SECONDARY · ADULT · LIBRARY

A Harcourt Company

www.steck-vaughn.com

Acknowledgments

Editorial Director: Stephanie Muller
Senior Editor: Kristy Schulz
Associate Director of Design: Cynthia Ellis
Design Manager: Alexandra Corona
Production Coordinator: Rebecca Gonzales
Media Researcher: Claudette Landry
Page Production Artist: Dina Bahan
Cover Production Artist: Alan Klemp

Cartography: Pp. 4–5, 7, 15, 23, 31, 39, 47, 55, 63, 71, 79, 87, 95, MapQuest.com, Inc.
Illustration Credits: Pp. 13, 21, 29, 37, 45, 53, 69, 77, 85, Eulala Conner
Photo Credits: Cover (background) ©Buddy Mays/CORBIS; front cover (inset) ©PhotoDisc; back cover (spot) ©Roger Ressmeyer/CORBIS; p.6 ©Don Mason/The Stock Market; pp.8-9 CORBIS/Bettmann-UPI; p.10 ©Charles & Josette Lenars/CORBIS; p.14 ©Gary Williams/Liaison Agency; p.16 ©Sipa Press; p.17 AP/Wide World Photos; p.18 ©Marilyn Yee/NYT Pictures; p.22 ©Les Stone/Sygma; p.24 ©Mark Downey/Liaison Agency; p.25 ©Thomas Van Dyke/San Jose Mercury News/Sygma; p.26 San Francisco Chronicle; p.30 ©John. M. Roberts/The Stock Market; p.32 ©Wolfgang Kaehler/CORBIS; p.33 ©Keith Gunnar/FPG International; p.34 ©Dale Wittner; p.38 ©Kelly-Mooney Photography/CORBIS; p.40(t) Courtesy Nicolas Estiverne; pp.40(b), 41 Reuters/Carole Devillers/Archive Photos; p.42 Reuters/Peter Andrews/Archive Photos; p.46 ©Pauline Horton; Papilio/CORBIS; p.48(t) AP/Wide World Photos; p.48(b) Courtesy the Hamada Family; pp.49-50 ©John Walker/The Fresno Bee; pp.54-58 AP/Wide World Photos; p.62 ©Jim Sugar Photography/CORBIS; p.64 ©Kevin P. Casey/Los Angeles Times Photo; p.65 ©John Mapanglo/Sipa Press; p.66 ©Robert Gauthier/Los Angeles Times Photo; p.70 ©AFP/CORBIS; pp.72-73 Sipa Press; p.74 ©AFP/CORBIS; p.78 ©Tony Stone Images/Marc Muench; p.80 Reuters/Jeff Mitchell/Archive Photos; p.81 ©Andrew Brown; Ecoscene/CORBIS; p.82 ©PA Photos; p.86 ©Galen Rowell/CORBIS; pp.88-90 ©AP/Wide World Photos; p.94 ©Alfred/Sipa Press; p.96 ©Eyup Coskum/Sipa Press; p.97 ©Daher/Liaison Agency; p.98 ©Alfred/Sipa Press; p.108(t) ©Les Stone/Sygma; p.108(m) ©Douglas Faulkner/Photo Researchers, Inc.; p.108(b) ©Bettmann/CORBIS; p.109(t) ©Galen Rowell/CORBIS; p.109(m) ©Reuters/John Kuntz/Archive Photos; p.109(b) ©John Zimmerman/FPG International.

Contents

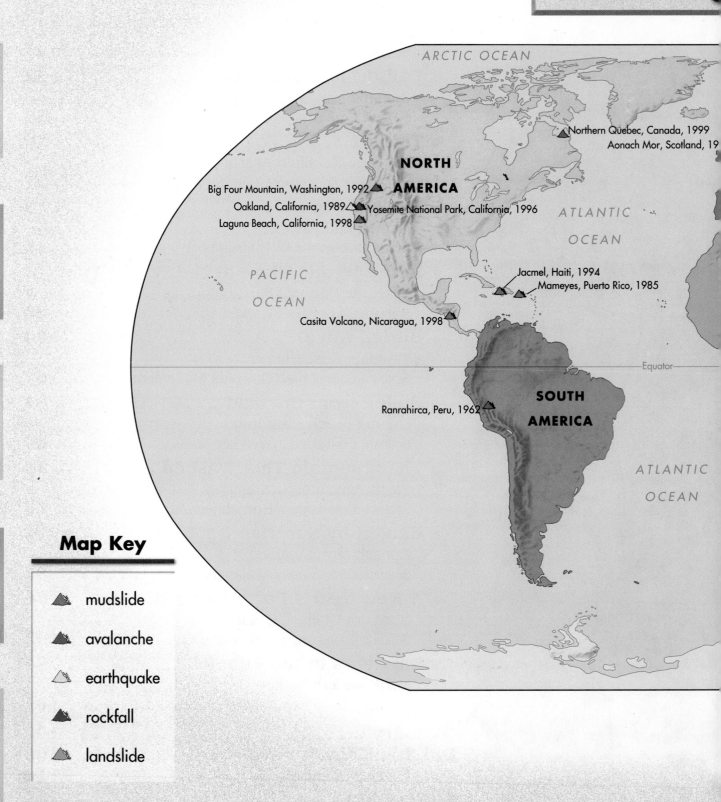

ARCTIC OCEAN

Northern Quebec, Canada, 1999
Aonach Mor, Scotland, 19

NORTH AMERICA

Big Four Mountain, Washington, 1992
Oakland, California, 1989
Laguna Beach, California, 1998
Yosemite National Park, California, 1996

ATLANTIC OCEAN

PACIFIC OCEAN

Jacmel, Haiti, 1994
Mameyes, Puerto Rico, 1985

Casita Volcano, Nicaragua, 1998

Equator

SOUTH AMERICA

Ranrahirca, Peru, 1962

ATLANTIC OCEAN

Map Key

🔺 mudslide

🔺 avalanche

🔺 earthquake

🔺 rockfall

🔺 landslide

ARCTIC OCEAN

EUROPE

ASIA

△ Turkey, 1999

Sea of

PACIFIC
OCEAN

FRICA

INDIAN
OCEAN

AUSTRALIA

Thredbo, Australia, 1997
△

N
W   E
S

ANTARCTICA

Danger from Above

At exactly 6 P.M., Alfonso Caballero stepped out the door of his home. Caballero was mayor of Ranrahirca, Peru. He enjoyed taking walks near his small town. On this night, January 10, 1962, Caballero chose to walk near the Santa River.

"Good evening," he called to a friend named Ricardo Olivera. But it wasn't going to be a good evening. High above the town, a **disaster** was taking shape. Within minutes, there would no longer be a town of Ranrahirca.

Trouble Coming

As Caballero walked, he paid no attention to the mountains above him. One of those mountains was Mount Huascarán. At 22,205 feet, it is the highest mountain in Peru. That year more snow had fallen on it than usual. Many townspeople said Mount Huascarán had never looked more beautiful.

But the extra snow caused a problem. As the weather turned warm, all that snow began to melt. Icy water dripped onto a **glacier** near the top of the mountain. The sheet of ice that formed the glacier was huge. It hung over the edge of a steep cliff. The dripping water **seeped** into the cracks of the glacier. As Caballero took his walk, a huge piece of the icy glacier suddenly broke off. It tumbled down the side of the mountain right toward Ranrahirca. As the enormous piece of ice tumbled, it grew in size. Soon it was 40 feet high and 1,000 yards wide. That made it higher than a two-story house and as wide as ten football fields.

The **massive** block of ice swept up everything in its path. It plowed up snow. The block of ice sent rocks, trees, and mud tumbling down the **slope**. Nothing could stop this growing **avalanche**.

The End of the World

As he walked out of town, Caballero saw what looked like a cloud near the top of the mountain. A few other people saw the same thing. Dr. Leoncio Guzmán was on his way home to Ranrahirca from a nearby hospital. He noticed the cloud near the top of Mount Huascarán. It looked golden in the sun's light. Then he realized it was no cloud. Said Guzmán, "I saw that the cloud was flying downhill...."

Most people in Ranrahirca never saw a thing. They were going about their business as usual. Shepherds were taking care of their sheep. Farmers were working in their fields. Children were playing outside.

Only as the avalanche neared the town did people sense danger. They heard a terrible roar. Some ran toward the church. They hoped to be safe there. A few ran toward the edge of town.

The avalanche buried the town of Ranrahirca in snow, mud, and ice.

A young girl looks at what is left of her small town.

One person who ran out of town was Lamberto Guzmán Tapia. He was at a family party with 40 people. Since Tapia was a mountain climber, he knew what the sound meant. He shouted a warning to the other guests. But no one seemed to hear him. He tried to warn the others again but they just kept talking and singing. "Save yourselves!" he finally shouted. Then he ran out the door as fast as he could.

Lamberto Guzmán Tapia ran in the right direction. He ran until he was out of town. Somehow he managed to get out of the way of the deadly avalanche. Another **survivor** was Zoila Cristina Angel. She was on high ground above the town when the avalanche struck.

"I saw it sweep by like a river, carrying away one farmer after another," she said.

Zoila heard someone shout, "Run! Run!"

"But I could not run," she said. "I could not move. I could not speak. I just looked at that awful thing that came rushing at us like the end of the world."

A Town Wiped Off the Map

Ricardo Olivera saw the avalanche just before it hit the town. By then the melting snow and ice had mixed with dirt, making mud. Olivera grabbed two young girls who were near him. He tried to pull them out of the way. But the wall of mud ripped them from his arms. Somehow Olivera **survived**. He was the only one in his family of 27 who did.

Mayor Caballero was still standing by the river when the avalanche hit the town. There was nothing he could do. In just a few seconds, the town was buried in ice and mud. As Caballero later said, "Ranrahirca was wiped off the map."

Ranrahirca was not the only town buried by the avalanche. Several smaller towns were also **destroyed**. The final **death toll** was more than 3,500 people. It was one of the worst avalanches in history.

In time, Caballero and other survivors began to look to the future. Caballero announced plans to build a new town. It, too, would be called Ranrahirca. The main street would be named the Street of January Tenth. In this way, the mayor hoped, the dead would never be forgotten.

The avalanche destroyed many towns that were in its path.

Read and Remember — Choose the Answer

Draw a circle around the correct answer.

1. What was Caballero doing when the avalanche hit?
   talking to a friend   taking a walk   taking a nap

2. On what mountain did the avalanche occur?
   Mt. Huascarán   Mt. Guzmán   Mt. Peru

3. What did the avalanche look like from far away?
   rain   a cloud   a rock

4. What did people hear just before the avalanche hit?
   a terrible roar   a long whistle   a loud scream

5. What swept through the center of town?
   a big rock   a giant snowball   a wall of mud

6. How many people died in the avalanche?
   less than 50   about 150   more than 3,500

Think About It — Find the Main Ideas

Underline the two most important ideas from the story.

1. Alfonso Caballero was mayor of Ranrahirca.

2. Some people ran to the church, hoping to find safety there.

3. Ranrahirca was destroyed by an avalanche.

4. The Santa River was near the town of Ranrahirca.

5. Forty people were at a family party when the avalanche hit.

6. The avalanche struck without much warning.

Focus on Vocabulary — Find the Meaning

Read each sentence. Circle the best meaning for the word in dark print.

1. No one knew a **disaster** was about to take place.

terrible event   exciting party   small storm

2. The **glacier** was huge.

center of town   ball of mud   sheet of ice

3. Water **seeped** into the cracks.

poured quickly   flowed slowly   disappeared

4. The **massive** block of ice tumbled down the mountain.

cold   bright and shiny   very large

5. Mud, rocks, and trees slid down the **slope**.

slanted ground   road   edge of the river

6. Nothing could stop this growing **avalanche**.

rock   mountain of dirt   sliding snow and mud

7. Zoila Cristina Angel was one **survivor**.

rescue worker   person who lived   angry person

8. Somehow Ricardo Olivera **survived**.

stayed alive   ran away   gave up

9. Several towns were **destroyed**.

given warnings   completely ruined   very surprised

10. The **death toll** was high.

sadness   number of people who died   hope

Forming Mountains

Earth's rocky outer layer is called the **crust**. Changes in Earth's crust can form mountains. The diagrams below show four ways that a mountain can form. Study the diagrams. Write the answer to each question.

Volcanic Mountains

Melted rock pours up through cracks in the crust and hardens into a mountain.

Dome Mountains

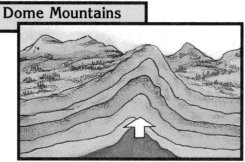

Melted rock pushes up rock layers into a dome shape.

Fold Mountains

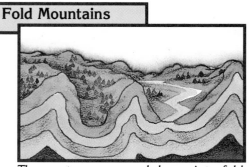

The crust squeezes rock layers into folds.

Block Mountains

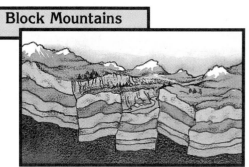

Land is pushed up along cracks in the crust.

1. What is Earth's outer layer called? _____

2. How are block mountains formed? _____

   _____

3. Which type of mountain is formed because Earth's crust squeezes rock layers? _____

4. Which two mountain types are formed by melted rock? _____

   _____

5. Which two mountain types are formed because of cracks in Earth's crust? _____

13

A Dangerous Hill

No one should have built any houses on the **hillside** called Mameyes. It was far too steep. But many poor people in Puerto Rico had no choice. They did not have the money to live in a safer place. By 1985, more than 1,500 people had moved to this hillside area in the city of Ponce. They were living in houses made out of wood and tin. For a while there was no problem. But when heavy rains came, the danger of living on the hill became clear.

A Hard Rain

Jesús Villegas Torres lived in Mameyes. He didn't like living there. But he never thought it was **risky**. He said, "The thought of danger never really passed through my mind."

Then on October 5, 1985, a weather **front** moved in. The front developed where warm air and cold air met. Soon the front brought a terrible, strong storm. It was called "**Tropical Storm** Isabel." For three days heavy rain fell. By the second day, Torres had started to worry. He wondered just how safe his little house was.

Others were also worried. One man from Mameyes was working in New York. He called his wife back home to make sure she was all right. "It was raining so hard there that we could barely hear each other," he said.

By the night of October 6, close to 15 inches of rain had fallen on Mameyes. Flooding was not a problem since the water ran off the 700-foot hill. But the hill itself was not **stable**. All the rain was loosening the soil.

The mud swept away many houses as it slid downhill.

When Jesús Villegas Torres went to bed that night, he was quite nervous. Then, in the middle of the night, he heard the sound of rocks hitting his tin roof. His neighbors were throwing rocks to wake him up. Torres ran out his front door. He heard people yelling, "Get out. All the houses are coming down. Grab your kids. Get out."

The neighbors were right. At 2:15 A.M., on October 7, the hillside began to crumble. The hard gray **limestone** soil just seemed to peel away. As the soil slid downhill, it carried many homes with it. Many people were still in their homes. They did not have a chance to get out. The moving soil took everything and everyone with it.

Torres looked around to see if anyone needed help. He saw part of a small house being crushed between a large **utility** pole and a wall. A woman was trapped inside. Torres and a friend ran over and broke a window. He and the friend grabbed the woman and dragged her to safety.

Getting Out

The **mudslide** swept away all the houses in its path. Yet not everyone died. "I cannot explain how we are alive," said Julio Maldonado. He, his wife, and their six children were trapped inside their house. "First the entrance wall fell off," said Maldonado. "Then the other walls fell off. Then we were sliding down, sandwiched between the floor and the ceiling." Somehow the whole family lived.

Nearby, William and Lilian Echevaria also survived. The **cement** floor of their home cracked wide open. Mud flowed up to their waists. Luckily, they managed to get out before the whole house sank.

Others were not so lucky. Miguel Santiago woke up when he felt his house move. "There was a crack, and everyone started screaming," he said. Santiago, his wife, and his mother jumped out a window. They scrambled to safety. But Santiago's 16-year-old sister was trapped on the bottom floor of the house. She didn't make it out.

The same thing happened to Saul Torres's family. When 16-year-old Saul woke up, he saw the walls of

After the mudslide, rescue workers searched for survivors.

his house splitting open. His bedroom was on the second floor. Thinking fast, he wrapped his legs around his 11-year-old brother, Nilson. The two boys held onto a mattress. They slid out of the house on the mattress and then climbed out of the mud. Their two sisters, however, were trapped on the first floor. They never had a chance.

Caught Under the Mud

Hundreds of others also died in the mudslide. Their bodies were found at the bottom of the hill, buried under 40 feet of mud. Many never knew what hit them. The mud filled every opening. There were no pockets of air for a trapped person to breathe. So anyone caught under the mud died quickly.

One man said the hill looked like a sand castle with one side washed away. Most of the houses had crashed to the bottom. Rafael Hernandez Colon, Governor of Puerto Rico, put it simply. He called it "the worst **tragedy** to ever strike the island." Said the governor sadly, "It fills me with pain."

Survivors hold each other after the terrible mudslide.

Read and Remember — Check the Events

Place a check in front of the three sentences that tell what happened in the story.

_____ **1.** People in Mameyes built big stone houses.

_____ **2.** A storm brought heavy rain to Mameyes.

_____ **3.** Many people left the hillside and moved to New York.

_____ **4.** Sliding mud swept away many houses in Mameyes.

_____ **5.** Hundreds of people died.

_____ **6.** Miguel Santiago pulled twenty people out of the mud.

Write About It

Imagine that you survived the mudslide in Mameyes. Write a paragraph telling people why they should not build new houses on the hillside.

Focus on Vocabulary — Make a Word

Choose a word in dark print to complete each sentence. Write the letters of the word on the blanks. When you are finished, the letters in the circles will tell where Mameyes is located.

hillside	**tropical**	**front**	**cement**	**risky**
limestone	**mudslide**	**stable**	**tragedy**	**utility**

1. "Isabel" was the name of a _____ storm. ○ _ _ _ _ _ _ _

2. Hundreds of people died in the _____. ○ _ _ _ _ _ _ _

3. The moving ground was not _____. ○ _ _ _ _ _ _

4. Mameyes was a _____ place to live. ○ _ _ _ _ _

5. A small house was crushed by a _____ pole. ○ _ _ _ _ _ _ _

6. The hard, gray soil was made of _____. _ _ _ ○ _ _ _ _ _

7. The _____ took place on October 7, 1985. ○ _ _ _ _ _ _

8. The _____ was very steep and muddy. ○ _ _ _ _ _ _ _ _

9. The Echevarias' _____ floor cracked open. ○ ○ _ _ _ _ _

10. The rain came when a weather _____ moved in. ○ _ _ _ _

Fronts

An **air mass** is a large body of air. When air masses with different **temperatures** meet, a **front** forms between them. In a cold front, a cold air mass pushes a warm air mass upward. In a warm front, a warm air mass moves over a cold air mass. Study the diagrams of fronts below. Write the answer to each question.

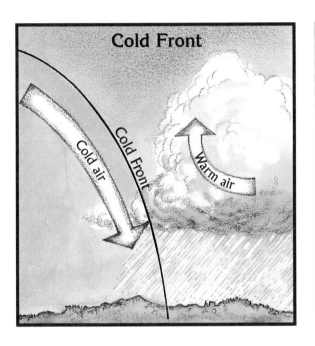

1. What is an air mass? _____

2. What forms between two air masses that meet each other?

   _____

3. Does rain usually occur in a warm front, a cold front, or both?

   _____

4. In which front does a cold air mass push up a warm air mass?

   _____

5. Does warm air rise above or sink below cold air?

   _____

California Earthquake

Bill McElroy lived right near the Nimitz Freeway in Oakland, California. From his house he could hear the steady hum of traffic. But it wasn't traffic that made his house shake on October 17, 1989. It was an **earthquake**. Deep inside the earth, gases and hot rocks were moving around. That caused the ground to shake very hard. At 5:04 P.M., an earthquake hit the cities of San Francisco and Oakland. It only lasted twenty seconds. But by the time it was over, the Nimitz Freeway was destroyed.

It Looked Like Something from a War

Bill McElroy was home when the earthquake hit. Quickly he ran for a doorway. He knew that was the safest place to stand.

The earthquake was a bad one. All earthquakes are measured using the **Richter scale**. On this scale, stronger earthquakes are given higher numbers. Anything over 6.0 is big trouble. This earthquake measured 7.1.

McElroy was lucky. His house was not ruined. When the ground stopped shaking, he ran outside to look around. That's when he saw dust and smoke rising from the nearby freeway.

McElroy hopped into his car. He raced to the freeway. When he got there, he stared in shock. The highway looked like something out of a war movie. There were twisted pieces of metal and small fires everywhere. The smoke was thick and heavy. McElroy could hardly see. He said, "It was pitch black."

McElroy soon realized part of the freeway had **collapsed**. The freeway had two levels. The top one had been about 70 feet above ground. The earthquake had caused this top level to collapse. Huge chunks of road had fallen down onto the lower level.

Some of the cars on the lower level had been crushed to just two or three feet high. The people inside were dead. Other cars were only partly crushed. The people inside these cars were trapped but still alive. McElroy could hear some of them crying for help.

Help Comes

In less than a minute, a crowd gathered at the freeway. Most people just looked at the **wreckage** in silence. They didn't know what to do. But Bill McElroy did. "We better get **organized**," he said. "There's people up there that need us."

McElroy wanted to climb up onto the freeway. He wanted to get survivors to safety before more of the road collapsed. But it wouldn't be easy. Even the

The earthquake caused the upper level of the freeway to collapse.

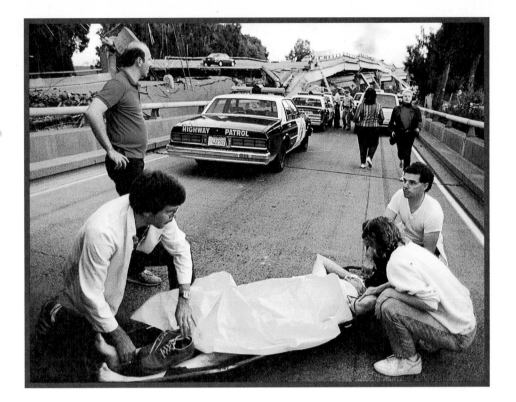

These people are helping an earthquake victim.

lower level of the freeway was 40 feet above the ground. "Go home and get ladders and some rope!" McElroy shouted. "Bring me some wire cutters, jacks, power saws, any tools you've got."

About 50 people rushed to do as McElroy asked. These people came from the nearby **community**. None of them had any training in rescue work. They just wanted to do what they could. They were willing to risk their lives to help strangers in trouble.

Soon McElroy and his neighbors were scrambling up onto the freeway. They held cloths over their mouths to keep out the dust and smoke. Holding flashlights, they went from car to car, checking for survivors. They found about 30 people.

They cut away metal and glass to get these people free. Then they helped get them to the ground. Some survivors slid down long ropes. Others climbed down ladders. Everyone worked as a **unit**. "The community was really pulling together," said McElroy. "The **official** people weren't even there yet."

Happy Endings, Sad Endings

One person who was saved by McElroy's **volunteers** was Lucy Adams. She was lying on the lower level of the freeway with a broken leg. As she looked over the edge of the road, she saw a man standing below her. "Go on, jump," the man shouted. "I'll break your fall." Adams took a deep breath and did as he said. The man caught her. Then he carried her to a second man who rushed her to the hospital.

Not all the volunteers' efforts had happy endings. Don Rich heard a child's cry. He tried **desperately** to find the child. But he couldn't. At one point Rich pulled a man out of a car. Only after he dragged him away did he realize the man was dead.

Still, McElroy and the others were a big help. They kept working even after firefighters arrived. By 11:00 P.M., it looked as though all the survivors had been found. Still, some volunteers searched through the night. Others came back the next day to offer more help.

In all, the earthquake killed 62 people. But it could have been worse. Others could have died. But they didn't, thanks in part to Bill McElroy and other members of the community.

Lucy Adams was lucky to be alive after the freeway collapsed.

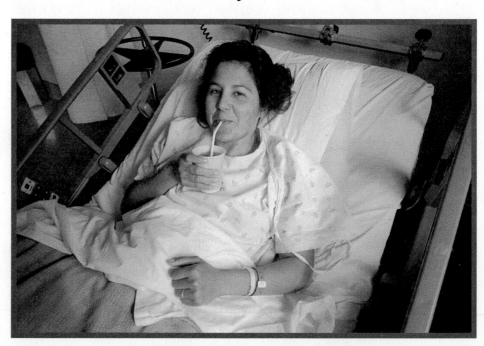

Read and Remember — Finish the Sentence

Circle the best ending for each sentence.

1. Bill McElroy lived very near the _____.
   freeway   desert   airport

2. McElroy asked his neighbors to bring him some _____.
   bandages   tools   dry clothes

3. Some people were trapped inside their _____.
   homes   tents   cars

4. McElroy and his neighbors searched for _____.
   survivors   money   police officers

5. McElroy and his neighbors kept working even after _____ arrived.
   teachers   firefighters   helicopters

6. When Lucy Adams jumped off the freeway, a man _____ her.
   shouted at   caught   dragged

Think About It — Drawing Conclusions

Write one or more sentences to answer each question.

1. Why did McElroy drive to the freeway? _____

   _____

2. Why did Lucy Adams jump off the freeway? _____

   _____

3. Why did McElroy want ladders and rope? _____

   _____

4. Why did McElroy tell his neighbors what to do? _____

   _____

Focus on Vocabulary — Finish the Paragraphs

Use the words in dark print to complete the paragraphs. Reread the paragraphs to be sure they make sense.

Richter scale	**collapsed**	**organized**	**earthquake**
community	**volunteers**	**desperately**	**official**
wreckage	**unit**		

Bill McElroy was at home in Oakland, California. On October 17, 1989, a terrible **(1)**_____ struck. It measured 7.1 on the **(2)**_____. The earthquake was a big one. Part of the Nimitz Freeway near McElroy's house **(3)**_____.

McElroy drove quickly to the Nimitz Freeway to look at the **(4)**_____. Many people were killed. Others there were hurt. They **(5)**_____ needed help. So McElroy quickly **(6)**_____ rescue efforts. He asked people to help. About 50 people from his **(7)**_____ agreed to risk their lives to help others. They were not paid. They were **(8)**_____. These people all worked together as a **(9)**_____. The volunteers rescued many people before the **(10)**_____ rescue workers arrived on the scene.

Earthquakes

Large pieces of Earth's rocky **crust** are always moving. They move past one another along a **fault**, or long crack. When the crust pieces move suddenly, an **earthquake** can occur. The diagram below shows how an earthquake occurs. Study the diagram. Write the answer to each question.

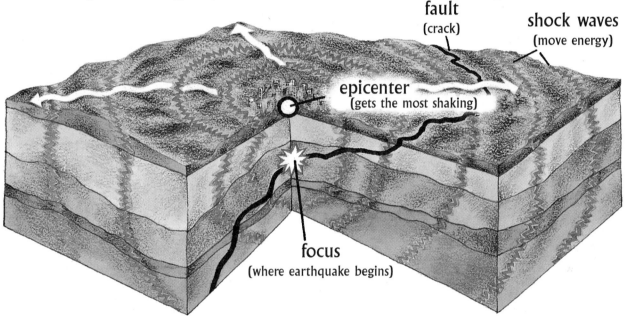

1. What is a long crack in Earth's crust called? _____

2. Where does an earthquake begin? _____

   _____

3. What is the point on the top of the ground that gets the most shaking during an earthquake? _____

   _____

4. What causes an earthquake? _____

   _____

5. What type of waves move energy during an earthquake?

   _____

Trouble at Big Four Mountain

obin Peterson wanted to go hiking. She didn't plan to take a hard trail. She was expecting her first child in six weeks. She just wanted an easy walk in the fresh air. So on January 4, 1992, she and her husband David decided to take a mile-long hike up to Big Four Mountain. This 6,135-foot peak is part of Washington's Cascade Mountain Range. Robin didn't want to climb the mountain. She only wanted to reach the base. She never dreamed it would be risky to do that.

Louder Than Thunder

At 2:05 P.M. Robin and David Peterson began their hike. Snow was falling all around them. They headed through a forest of **evergreen** trees. Two friends, Vaughn Rodewald and Mike Kichline, went with them. The men were excited. They hoped to explore the **ice caves** at the bottom of the mountain.

David Peterson and Vaughn Rodewald had first seen the ice caves a month earlier. The caves were huge. They were made out of snow left by an avalanche. Water and wind had **hollowed** out deep holes in the snow. **Forest rangers** warned people not to go into the caves. The walls could collapse at any time. But many people went in anyway. They wanted to see what the inside of the caves looked like.

The Petersons and their friends got to the bottom of Big Four Mountain at 3:30 P.M. By then, Robin was ready for a rest. She agreed to wait outside the ice cave while the men went in.

David Peterson, Vaughn Rodewald, and Mike Kichline squeezed through the cave's narrow entrance. They turned on flashlights and looked around. They couldn't believe how big the cave was. Farther and farther in they walked. After 15 minutes, they were about 500 feet from the cave's entrance. Suddenly, they heard a loud noise.

"It was really, really loud," said David Peterson. "Louder than thunder. It was **deafening**." The men guessed that an avalanche had fallen right at the entrance to the cave. Forty **tons** of heavy snow now lay between them and the outside world.

Swept Away

Robin Peterson had no warning that the avalanche was coming. One minute she was looking around enjoying the view. The next minute she was being swept off her feet by a huge wave of snow. "I had this feeling of being thrown around like a helpless rag doll," she said. "I don't remember any pain, just complete **confusion**."

The snow carried her 200 feet. She ended up on the other side of a big field. Her glasses had been lost in the snow. She could barely see. But Robin knew that her husband and friends were trapped inside the ice cave. She said, "All I could think about was David and that I had to get help."

Robin struggled to her feet. With tears running down her face, she stumbled through the snow. She headed back through the forest toward the road. Robin was tired and scared. She had a **bruise** on her head. But she kept going. It was getting dark and she wanted to get help as quickly as possible.

A Lesson Learned

Meanwhile, her husband and friends were trying to dig themselves out of the cave. "We knew we were in deep," said Vaughn Rodewald. "We just didn't know how deep."

Rodewald began digging through the snow that blocked their path. At first he used his gloved hands. But he knew that digging by hand would take too long. So he switched to a three-inch camping knife. He used the blade to cut blocks out of the snow. This allowed Rodewald to move through the snow faster. Little by little he cut a narrow tunnel.

An avalanche carries tons of snow as it moves downhill.

David Peterson and Mike Kichline waited in the cave behind him. David was worried about his wife. "I couldn't stop thinking about Robin," he said. "Was she alive? Was the baby okay?"

At one point David tried to help dig the tunnel. But he hated small places. The two-foot-wide tunnel was too small for him. He began to **panic**. Rodewald calmed him down while Mike Kichline took over digging with the knife.

Kichline dug for two hours. At last he saw light up ahead. He had reached the open air! Quickly he and the other men crawled out to freedom.

By then, hikers had met Robin Peterson on the trail. They had called for help. Robin had been taken to a nearby hospital where she learned that she and the baby were going to be fine. By the time rescue workers got to the cave, they found the men safely outside.

David Peterson rushed to the hospital. He fell into Robin's arms in tears. He was thankful that she and the baby were doing well. Later he admitted he should never have gone into the ice cave. "It was stupid of us," he said. "We've **definitely** learned our lesson."

Later the Petersons, Kichline, and two others returned to the mountain.

Read and Remember — Choose the Answer

Draw a circle around the correct answer.

1. Why did people go into the ice caves?

   to get warm   to look around   to hide

2. Where was Robin while her husband was in the ice cave?

   in the car   outside the cave   at the top of the mountain

3. What did Robin lose in the avalanche?

   her glasses   her car keys   her shoes

4. What did the men use to dig through the snow?

   a shovel   a camping knife   their bare hands

5. Why was it so hard for David to be trapped in the ice cave?

   He was hurt.   He hated small spaces.   He was cold.

Write About It

Imagine you had survived being trapped in the ice cave with David Peterson, Vaughn Rodewald, and Mike Kichline. Write a paragraph telling what you would do to warn others about going inside ice caves.

Focus on Vocabulary — Match Up

Match each word with its meaning. Darken the circle beside the correct answer.

1. evergreen
   ○ terribly loud   ○ a long time   ○ always has green leaves

2. ice caves
   ○ big holes in snow   ○ unheated cabins   ○ mountains

3. hollowed
   ○ carved out   ○ shouted   ○ greeted softly

4. forest rangers
   ○ hikers   ○ firefighters   ○ people who protect the forest

5. deafening
   ○ very cold   ○ very quiet   ○ very loud

6. tons
   ○ units of weight   ○ truckloads   ○ metal barrels

7. confusion
   ○ feeling pain   ○ not being sure   ○ talking too much

8. bruise
   ○ large cut   ○ hurt skin that looks blue   ○ bright light

9. panic
   ○ take deep breaths   ○ cry softly   ○ feel very frightened

10. definitely
    ○ never   ○ without doubt   ○ not sure

Mountain Plants

Plant life and air change at different heights of a mountain. For example, a cold, snowy mountaintop has few plants. The diagram below shows a mountain. Study the diagram. Write the answer to each question.

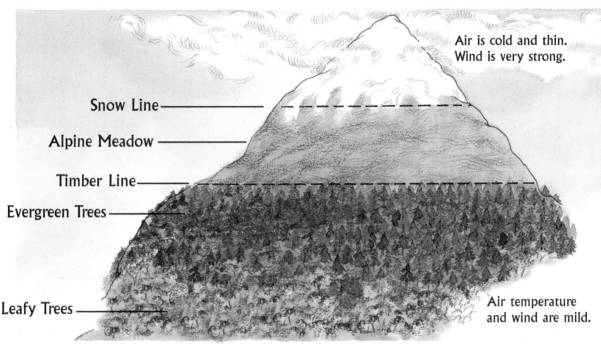

Snow Line

Alpine Meadow

Timber Line

Evergreen Trees

Leafy Trees

Air is cold and thin. Wind is very strong.

Air temperature and wind are mild.

1. What is the line at which trees can no longer grow?

_____

2. What is the name of the grassy area below the snow line?

_____

3. How do air and wind change at the top of a mountain?

_____

_____

4. What are two kinds of trees that grow below the timber line?

_____

5. Do plants grow well above the snow line? _____

Mudslide in Haiti

icholas Estiverne was worried. Tropical Storm Gordon was headed for Haiti, a country in the Caribbean Sea. Estiverne was a lawyer in the United States. But he had been born in Haiti. He had friends there. He hoped the country would not be hit too hard by the storm.

Soon Estiverne got bad news. On November 13, 1994, the storm hit Haiti. Estiverne knew what that meant. The rain from the storm would cause mudslides. The mudslides would bring big trouble for Haiti.

No Warning

Most people living in Haiti didn't even know a storm was coming. Haiti is a very poor country. Most Haitians live in huts with no electricity. They have no TVs or radios. They have no phones, either. So no warnings could reach them.

Tropical Storm Gordon hit Haiti on the morning of November 13. By that evening, high winds and driving rain were blasting the small country. More than one foot of rain fell. Homes became flooded. Some people climbed onto rooftops to keep from being washed away.

In the town of Jacmel, people **huddled** in their homes. But as Nicholas Estiverne knew, their houses were not safe. They were just "little mud houses," he said.

To make matters worse, many of these houses stood in the worst possible place. They had been built in a dry **riverbed** that ran through the center of town. "Many of the people had lived in the dry riverbed for years," said Estiverne. "The bed had been

Nicholas Estiverne

dry for so long that people **assumed** it was dry land." But now that heavy rain was falling, dirt in and around the riverbed was mixing with water. The whole riverbed was filling up with heavy, wet mud.

The riverbed was not the only place where mud was forming. The hillsides around Jacmel also were turning to mud. Much of the problem came from lack of trees. People had cut down almost all the trees on the hillsides. They had done that in order to get firewood. With no tree roots in the ground, nothing held the soil in place. The result was a lot of **erosion**. The dirt that was left on the hillsides was loose and dry. It mixed with rain to make rivers of mud.

Mudslide

All day the people of Jacmel waited for the sky to clear. But the rain kept getting heavier. Around midnight, waves of mud from the hillsides headed

Mud filled people's homes as it flowed down the hillsides.

Mud smashed many houses to pieces.

down toward Jacmel. As the mud flowed, it knocked over everything in its path. It pulled up bushes. It washed away roads and took out bridges. Gathering speed, the mudslide became bigger and bigger. Soon it was carrying 45 tons of mud and **debris**. The debris of broken boards, sticks, bushes, and rocks had mixed with the sliding mud.

The wave of mud came rushing into the center of Jacmel. The **rickety** houses in the riverbed stood no chance against the force of the mud. Some houses were buried by the mudslide. Others were smashed to pieces.

The people of Jacmel did not have much time to get out of the way. "Many of the kids ran away," Estiverne later reported. Some of them got thrown out of the mud and water and managed to find their way to higher ground. But as Estiverne said, "The parents were not able to get out as quickly. Some of the parents disappeared in the mud."

Offering Help

When the rain finally stopped, Jacmel was nearly destroyed. Many homes had been washed away. Hundreds of bodies lay buried under the mud. Everywhere children walked around, **dazed**. Overnight, they had become homeless. Many of them had lost both their parents.

Estiverne knew he could not bring the parents back. But he wanted to help these children in any way he could. So he started the Haitian Relief Fund. He gathered one ton of clothing and food. He also raised money to set up **orphanages**. "Haiti had to open nine orphanages as a **result** of the storm," Estiverne explained. "Each has 40 or 50 kids."

The people of Jacmel had **suffered** greatly because of Tropical Storm Gordon. But Nicholas Estiverne hoped the worst was behind them. He hoped that with his help, many Haitians would be able to build new and better lives.

The rain and mud left many people of Jacmel without homes.

Read and Remember — Check the Events

Place a check in front of the three sentences that tell what happened in the story.

_____ **1.** Tropical Storm Gordon just missed Haiti.

_____ **2.** The hillsides around Jacmel turned to mud.

_____ **3.** Many children were left without parents.

_____ **4.** Nicholas Estiverne started the Haitian Relief Fund.

_____ **5.** Many people climbed trees to escape the mud.

_____ **6.** Children and animals were able to swim through the mud.

Think About It — Fact or Opinion

A **fact** is a true statement. An **opinion** is a statement that tells what a person thinks. Write **F** beside each statement that is a fact. Write **O** beside each statement that is an opinion.

_____ **1.** Haiti is a nice place to live.

_____ **2.** Most Haitians have no phones.

_____ **3.** Nicholas Estiverne was a lawyer in the United States.

_____ **4.** Haitians should not be allowed to cut down trees.

_____ **5.** Some people climbed onto rooftops to stay safe.

_____ **6.** Nicholas Estiverne raised money to help Haitians.

_____ **7.** It is sometimes fun to play in mud.

_____ **8.** No one should live in Jacmel.

Focus on Vocabulary — Crossword Puzzle

Use the clues to complete the puzzle. Choose from the words in dark print.

result   debris   orphanages   suffered   dazed

erosion   huddled   riverbed   rickety   assumed

Across

1. caused by something
5. homes for children whose parents have died
6. land where a river flows or used to flow
9. not aware of things
10. lived in pain or sadness

Down

2. a process that wears away soil
3. thought something was a certain way
4. gathered close together
7. very shaky or about to fall apart
8. pieces of broken things

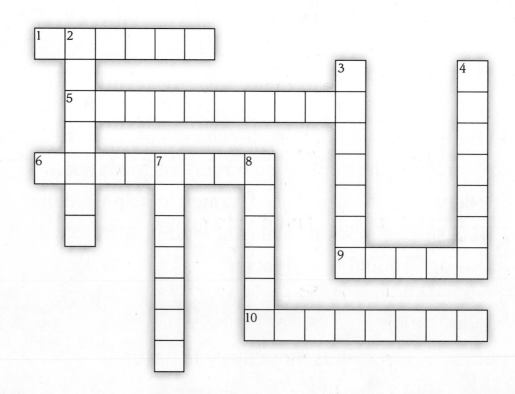

Mudslides

Without trees, **erosion** of the soil can occur easily. A **mudslide** due to heavy rain can be very dangerous. The diagram below shows some of the results of a mudslide. Study the diagram. Circle the word that best completes each sentence.

1. Trees help protect houses from _____.
burning   mudslides   creeks

2. The houses below the trees are _____ protected from mudslides.
most   least   not at all

3. Soil sliding down a mountain due to heavy rain is called _____.
a mudslide   a flood   erosion

4. Heavy rains can also cause _____.
floods   fires   snow

5. Without _____, erosion is more likely to occur.
trees   rain   mud

In the Wrong Place at the Wrong Time

isano Hamada wanted some ice cream. She got in line at the Happy Isle snack bar in California's Yosemite National Park. It was 7 P.M. on July 10, 1996. The snack bar was about to close. Hamada and her friend Kelly Booth were among the last customers of the day.

Suddenly, Hamada and Booth heard a loud noise. They didn't know what it was. But they knew it wasn't good. They dove behind the snack bar. As it turned out, that was not a safe place to hide.

Dust and Wind

A few weeks earlier, Hamada and Booth had finished high school in Whittier, California. They had come to the park with four other friends to relax. They planned to hike, camp, and have fun for another week. But all that changed on July 10th.

The noise the girls heard was caused by a falling rock. It was not just any old rock. This rock was massive. It measured over 300 feet long. The rock weighed 31,500 tons. It was made out of **granite**, a very hard kind of rock. It had been part of a cliff that rose high above the snack bar. When the rock broke loose, it fell 2,500 feet. Then it exploded on the floor of the valley below.

As the rock struck the ground, it sent up a big cloud of dust. Crushed bits of rock rose 1,000 feet in the air. The dust made it hard for anyone to see more than three or four feet. A man named Tom Brander was hiking nearby. He said, "I opened my eyes and I thought I was blind. The dust was so thick it blocked out the sun."

A huge rock fell from the cliff to the valley below.

The falling rock also caused a huge blast of wind. This blast was so strong it ripped trees up by their roots. At least 500 trees went flying through the air. Some of these trees were 250 feet tall. Picnic tables, too, went sailing through the air. The wind **damaged** a nearby nature center. It blew the Happy Isle snack bar to pieces.

Hit by Flying Trees

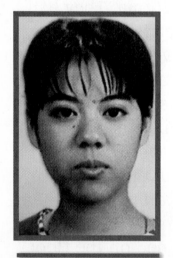

Hisano Hamada

The rock itself did not hit anyone. But the flying trees and other objects did. One tree fell on top of Emiliano Morales. He was one of Hisano Hamada's friends. The big tree crushed Morales to death.

Other trees hit Hamada and Booth. The girls were not killed, but they were hurt. Kelly Booth had cuts on her face and arms. There was one very deep cut over her right eye. Hamada was in much worse shape. She had a broken arm. She had leg **injuries**. Worst of all, her neck was broken.

Rescuers hurried to the area. But it wasn't easy for them to see. It took 45 minutes for the dust to settle. As it did, rescuers looked out over a terrible scene.

Fallen trees were stacked on top of one another. In some places these trees were ten deep. Dust covered 50 **acres**. That is a space about the size of five city blocks. The layer of dust was six inches deep.

Hamada and Booth were rushed to nearby hospitals. There, doctors **operated** on Hamada for six hours. It would take many months for her injuries to heal.

A Guessing Game

Meanwhile, rescuers kept searching through the **rubble**. They wanted to be sure they had found everyone. In all, fifteen people were hurt. It could have been much worse. The rock could have fallen when the snack bar was full. If the rock had broken off in the middle of the day, hundreds of people could have been hurt. "We would have had more blood than anyone could imagine," said park worker Jim Snyder.

The falling rock caused a huge blast of wind that snapped trees in half.

As it was, this was one of the worst **rockfalls** in the park's history. Falling rocks are common in Yosemite National Park. Most are small and hurt no one.

Like other rockfalls, this one started with a small crack. Rainwater flowed into a crack in the cliff above the snack bar. In the winter, this rainwater froze. In the spring, it melted again. The water put **pressure** on the crack. Over time, the crack got wider and wider. Finally, it got so wide that a part of the cliff broke off.

Park workers are always on the **lookout** for any rocks that might fall. They listen for the sound of rocks shifting. They watch for small rockfalls that might lead to larger ones. They keep a map of all rockfalls in the park.

Still, it is impossible for park workers to predict when or if a rockfall will happen. It is largely a guessing game. There was no way visitors to the park on July 10 could have known that the rock would fall. Hisano Hamada and her friends just happened to be in the wrong place at the wrong time.

The rockfall destroyed Yosemite's Happy Isle snack bar.

Read and Remember — Finish the Sentence

Circle the best ending for each sentence.

1. Hamada and Booth were in Yosemite National Park to _____.
   study rocks   have fun   work at the snack bar

2. The rock that fell was very _____.
   sharp   large   wet

3. When the rock hit the ground, it created a huge _____.
   cloud of dust   fire   avalanche

4. The wind destoyed the _____.
   snack bar   park gate   water tank

5. Hamada and Booth were hit by _____.
   glass   trees   a car

6. At first, rescuers had trouble _____.
   breathing   seeing   moving

Write About It

Imagine you are a newspaper reporter interviewing Hisano Hamada. Write three questions you would want to ask her.

1. _____
   _____

2. _____
   _____

3. _____
   _____

Focus on Vocabulary — Finish Up

Choose the correct word in dark print to complete each sentence.

damaged	**pressure**	**operated**	**lookout**	**injuries**
rubble	**rescuers**	**granite**	**rockfalls**	**acres**

1. To have harmed or broken something is to have _____ it.

2. A very hard kind of rock is _____ .

3. Doctors who have done surgery on someone have _____ on that person.

4. People who try to save those in trouble are called _____ .

5. To push or press against something is to put _____ on it.

6. When rocks break off and fall from cliffs or mountainsides, they are called _____ .

7. Cuts, scratches, and broken bones are examples of _____ .

8. Rough, broken pieces of stone and rock are called _____ .

9. Land is often measured in _____ .

10. To be watching for something is to be on the _____ .

Rockfalls

Sometimes ice can cause rocks to crack and break off cliffs. This is called **frost wedging**. The diagram below shows how frost wedging occurs. Study the diagram. Write the answer to each question.

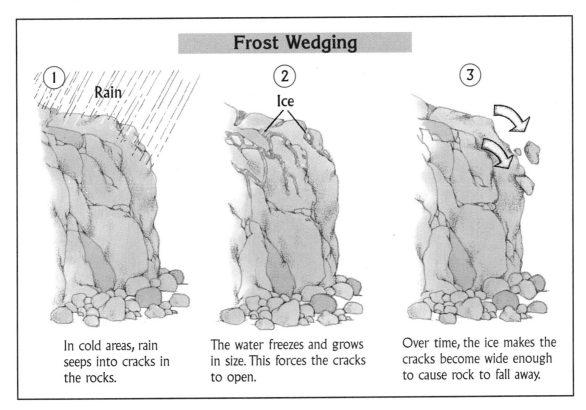

Frost Wedging

1 Rain

2 Ice

3

In cold areas, rain seeps into cracks in the rocks.

The water freezes and grows in size. This forces the cracks to open.

Over time, the ice makes the cracks become wide enough to cause rock to fall away.

1. What is the first step in frost wedging? _____

_____

2. What causes rocks to crack and break off cliffs? _____

3. When water freezes, does it shrink or grow in size? _____

4. How do cracks open farther and farther? _____

_____

5. Why do you think park workers worry about frost wedging?

_____

Buried Alive

Stuart and Sally Diver went to bed early on July 30, 1997. It had been a long and tiring day. Stuart had given ski lessons all day. He taught ski lessons at the Bimbadeen **Lodge** in Thredbo, Australia. Sally worked in a nearby hotel. By evening the Divers were tired out. They settled into their apartment on the ground floor of the Bimbadeen Lodge. By 9:00 P.M. they were fast asleep. They had no idea that their happy lives were about to be **shattered**.

No Time To Move

At 11:30 that night, a **landslide** began on the mountain above the Divers. Water from an **underground spring** had loosened much of the earth. That caused a huge part of the mountain to collapse. Dirt, rocks, snow, and trees suddenly came rolling down the mountain.

The noise woke Stuart. For a moment he thought a storm had kicked up. Then he thought a bomb had exploded. In any case, he had no time to move. He and Sally were still lying in bed when the landslide hit the lodge.

Instantly the building collapsed around them. The Divers were buried under 30 feet of rubble. Eighteen other people in the lodge were crushed to death. Stuart and Sally were not killed. But they were trapped under **concrete**. Three huge **slabs** of concrete lay on top of them. Two metal bars held up the slabs. If the bars broke, the slabs would crush the Divers. As it was, they couldn't move. They were pinned on their backs. One of the slabs was just inches from Stuart's face.

Alone in the Dark

Stuart and Sally lay screaming under the concrete. Then they heard another loud roar. A huge wave of water from the underground spring was rushing down the mountain.

"I could hear it coming, rolling down the hill like a train," Stuart Diver later said. "I started to pray that it would pass by, but it hit us. It was freezing." In just five seconds the water had covered Sal's face," said Stuart.

Stuart's face was almost covered, too. But he managed to lift his head a few inches. He pressed his nose against the concrete slab and tried to breathe. He stayed like that for 30 minutes. At last, the flow of water slowed down. But by then Sally Diver had drowned.

Now Stuart was all alone in the darkness. "He was in what we call cave darkness," rescue worker Paul Featherstone later said. "That's pure and **total** dark."

Rescue workers move a survivor of the landslide.

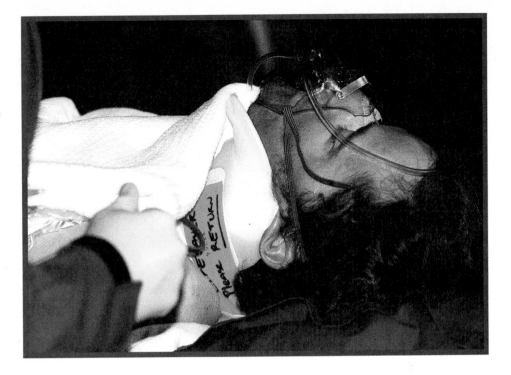

Stuart Diver is rushed to the hospital.

Stuart was cold, wet, and scared. All his life he had hated small spaces. Now it looked as though he was going to die in one. Yet Stuart held on to life.

Long Hours of Waiting

Rescue workers rushed to the scene. They didn't know if anyone had survived the landslide. But they began to dig through the rubble. It was tricky work. The ground was still not stable. Now and then more dirt and rocks fell from the mountain above.

Police brought in special instruments that can pick up body heat. The instruments showed no sign of life. Stuart was too far down under the debris and rubble to be **detected**.

Hour after hour the rescuers worked. During this time, Stuart developed **hypothermia**. That meant his body **temperature** was dropping dangerously low. His heart was beating slower. His whole body was shutting down. Eight times icy water flooded his tiny air space. Each time he survived only by pushing his face up against the slab.

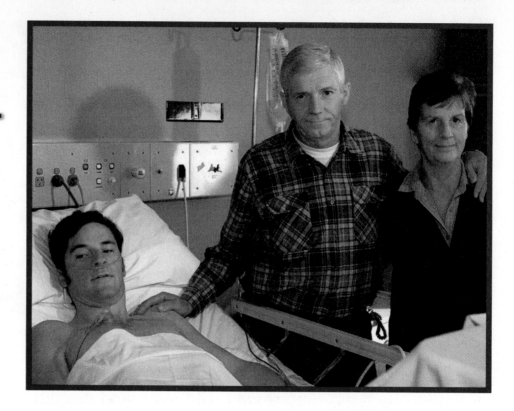

Diver was lucky to have survived the terrible landslide.

After many hours, Stuart heard the faint voices of rescuers high above him. He yelled out to them. At first, though, they could not hear him. Finally rescue worker Steve Hurst thought he had heard a sound coming from the rubble. He asked the other workers to be quiet. "Can anyone hear me?" he shouted.

Stuart felt a wave of joy fill his heart. He had been found! "I can hear you!" he shouted back.

Rescuers began to dig down to Stuart. They dug through dirt, rocks, and boards. But they couldn't reach him. He was still under the three concrete slabs. Each was nine inches thick. Carefully rescuers began to saw through the concrete. They hoped the slabs would not fall on Stuart.

The sawing took about ten hours. Finally, after 65 hours under the rubble, Stuart Diver was lifted to safety. Many rescuers couldn't believe he was still alive. Dr. Richard Morris had helped with the rescue. Morris said Stuart's chances of living through the landslide "were one in a million."

Read and Remember — Choose the Answer

Draw a circle around the correct answer.

1. Where did Stuart and Sally Diver live?

   America   Austria   Australia

2. Where were the Divers when the landslide struck?

   at a party   in bed   skiing down a mountain

3. What killed Sally Diver?

   water   poison   snow

4. What name did rescuers give to pure darkness?

   eye darkness   cave darkness   blind darkness

5. What happened to Stuart as he lay trapped?

   He became cold.   He lost his hearing.   An animal bit him.

Think About It — Cause and Effect

A **cause** is something that makes something else happen. What happens is called the **effect**. Match each cause with an effect. Write the letter on the correct blank. The first one is done for you.

Cause	Effect
1. The landslide hit quickly, so __e__	**a.** he asked the other rescuers to be quiet.
2. Stuart was in freezing water, so _____	**b.** he grew colder and colder.
3. The ground was not stable, so _____	**c.** they went to bed early.
4. Steve Hurst heard a sound below the rubble, so _____	**d.** rescuers had to work carefully.
5. The Divers were tired, so _____	**e.** the Divers had no time to get out.

Focus on Vocabulary — Finish the Paragraphs

Use the words in dark print to complete the paragraphs. Reread the paragraphs to be sure they make sense.

shattered	**landslide**	**Lodge**	**total**
temperature	**detected**	**concrete**	**slabs**
hypothermia	**underground spring**		

Stuart and Sally Diver lived in Thredbo, Australia. Their home was at the Bimbadeen **(1)**_____. Their lives were **(2)**_____ on July 30, 1997. That is when a **(3)**_____ struck. The Divers were trapped under three **(4)**_____ made out of **(5)**_____. Stuart and Sally were alive. Others in the lodge had been crushed to death.

Then freezing water from an **(6)**_____ flowed over them. Sally soon drowned. But Stuart managed to raise his head above the water. With Sally gone, Stuart was left alone in **(7)**_____ darkness. Stuart thought he was going to die, too. But Stuart yelled out for help whenever he could.

It was many hours before rescuers **(8)**_____ Stuart from under the rubble. By then, his body **(9)**_____ was quite low. He was suffering from **(10)**_____. Finally, after 65 hours, Stuart was lifted to safety.

Downhill Movement

Gravity is the force that pulls objects toward the earth. It causes rocks and soil to slide down a hill. The chart below describes different types of downhill movement. Study the chart. Write the answer to each question.

DOWNHILL MOVEMENT			
TYPE	DESCRIPTION	SPEED	CAUSE
landslide	Large amounts of soil and rock tumble down a hill or mountain.	fast	An earthquake, a volcano eruption, or heavy rain occurs, loosening rocks.
mudflow	Thick mud moves down a slope, picking up more soil and other objects.	fast	Heavy rain turns soil into mud, which slides downhill.
slump	A large block of rock slides downhill.	fast	A large block of rock breaks off and moves downhill.
earthflow	Soil and plants move slowly downhill.	slow	Heavy rain loosens and moves soil.
creep	Soil moves downhill over a long period of time.	very slow	The force of gravity moves soil materials.

1. What are three types of fast downhill movement? _____

_____

2. What are two types of slow downhill movement? _____

_____

3. What is an earthflow? _____

_____

4. What can cause a landslide? _____

_____

5. Which is the slowest type of downhill movement? _____

Pulled from the Mud

Teresa and Carmelo Sarabia were tired of the rain. All month the weather had been bad. Now, on February 23, 1998, yet more rain was pounding the California **coast**. Hour after hour heavy rain fell. Water **gushed** down the hill behind the Sarabias' apartment in Laguna Beach. At one point Teresa stepped outside to look at it. She hoped the rain would stop soon. Otherwise, she feared, the whole hillside might wash away.

Knocked Off Their Feet

That evening, the Sarabias put nine-month-old Tiffany to bed in her crib. Then they sat down to watch TV. Their other children, 20-year-old Efrain and 19-year-old Ivvone, were with them.

At 11:45 P.M., a loud roar filled the air. At the same time, all the lights went out. Frightened, Teresa ran to the crib. She **scooped** up Tiffany. With one arm she held the baby close to her body. With her other arm she reached for Carmelo. Efrain and Ivvone were also **terrified**. They ran into the bathroom.

As Teresa and Carmelo stood holding hands, a wall of mud crashed through the apartment. The hillside behind them had given way. The heavy **rainstorm** had soaked the dirt and turned it to mud. This wet mud was now rushing downhill, crashing into everything in its path.

Efrain and Ivvone were not carried away by the mud. But Teresa, Carmelo, and Tiffany were. Teresa tried to **shield** Tiffany against her body. But mud hit

Teresa with such force that it knocked her off her feet.
Carmelo was knocked over, too. Desperately Teresa
tried to hold on to her baby. "I had her in my arm,"
she said. "But then I went rolling down with her and
she was pulled away from me..."

A Ball of Mud

At last Teresa stopped rolling. She was covered
with mud. Pieces of wood lay over her, pinning her
to the ground. "My mouth was full of mud," she later
said. "I was cleaning it out so I could yell for help for
my baby." Carmelo lay a few feet away. He couldn't
move, either. He said, "The baby was crying. I could
hear her, but I couldn't see her."

Teresa and Carmelo fought to get free. But it was
no use. They were trapped under too much debris.
They had to hope someone would come help them
and their baby. "I kept yelling for someone to help
us," Carmelo said. But as Teresa and Carmelo waited,
Tiffany's cries stopped. Both parents feared their little
girl was dead.

As it turned out, Tiffany was not dead. But she was in trouble. The mud had carried her along, tossing her this way and that. At last it tossed her up onto a pile of rocks, branches, and broken furniture. By then, mud had filled her ears and mouth. She could no longer cry. She could barely breathe.

Luckily, she didn't stay that way long. A man named Gary Segraves spotted her. Like the Sarabias, Segraves had been caught in the mudslide. His glasses had come off so he couldn't see well. But as he lay on some rocks and twigs, he saw a ball of mud lying nearby. **Squinting**, he thought it was a doll. Then he wondered if it might be a child. "I pinched its fingers to see if it was alive," he said.

When he realized Tiffany was indeed alive, he grabbed her. He handed her to the first person he saw. That person was Todd Tingley, one of the Sarabias' neighbors. Tingley had also been caught in the mudslide and had survived. He was searching the rubble for other survivors.

Tingley looked into Tiffany's open eyes. Then he began to run down the road with her. He knew he had to get help for her fast. As he ran, he talked to her, telling her she would be all right.

A mudslide can destroy anything in its path.

Still Alive

Tingley headed straight for firefighter Frank Ybarra, who had just arrived. "I didn't have one foot on the ground when they handed me a baby covered in mud," Ybarra later said. "She had mud packed in her mouth and nose. She was very cold and wet, and she was not breathing."

Quickly Ybarra cleared Tiffany's nose and throat. "She started moaning a little bit. She was living!"

He cut off her mud-soaked pajamas and carried her into an ambulance. In that same ambulance lay Teresa Sarabia. She had been pulled from the mud and was about to be taken to the hospital. But she was screaming **frantically**. "My baby! My baby!" she cried. Ybarra held up Tiffany for her to see. Then mother and baby were rushed to the hospital.

Two people died in the mudslide that night. But **amazingly**, the whole Sarabia family survived. Teresa Sarabia knew much of the **credit** for that went to Gary Segraves. "My baby would've died had it not been for him," she said.

The Sarabia family finally were safe and together again.

Read and Remember — Check the Events

Place a check in front of the three sentences that tell what happened in the story.

_____ **1.** Heavy rain fell along the California coast.

_____ **2.** A mudslide washed away the Sarabias' church.

_____ **3.** Carmelo Sarabia died in the mud.

_____ **4.** Tiffany was swept out of her mother's arms.

_____ **5.** Gary Segraves rescued Tiffany from the mud.

_____ **6.** No one believed Teresa was Tiffany's mother.

Write About It

Imagine you are Efrain or Ivvone Sarabia. Write a paragraph describing how your parents and baby sister were rescued from the mudslide.

Focus on Vocabulary — Crossword Puzzle

Use the clues to complete the puzzle. Choose from the words in dark print.

scooped   gushed   amazingly   shield   rainstorm

coast   squinting   frantically   credit   terrified

Across

2. storm that brings rain
5. very frightened
7. acting out of control
8. picked up
9. flowed very quickly

Down

1. the land close to the sea
3. surprisingly
4. almost closing your eyes
6. praise or thanks
8. protect or cover

68

Weather Map

 A **weather map** shows what kind of weather to expect in an area. The **map key** explains what the symbols or colors on the map mean. The map below shows one day's weather in the United States. Study the map. Circle the answer to each question.

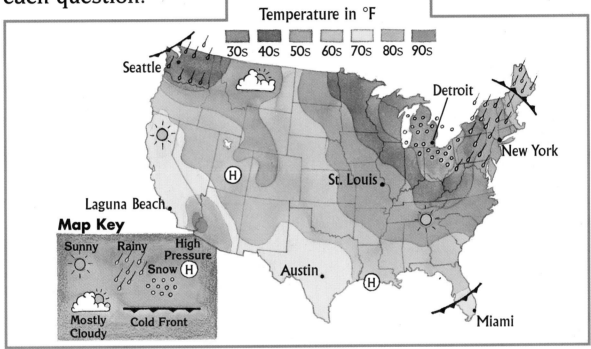

1. Which is the symbol for rain?

2. What color is used to show a temperature of 75°F?

   blue   dark orange   yellow

3. What is the weather like in Seattle?

   sunny   rainy   snowy

4. Which city should expect snow?

   New York   Detroit   Miami

5. Which city has about the same temperature as St. Louis?

   Laguna Beach   New York   Miami

The Mountain That Washed Away

The neighbors just laughed. They couldn't believe Pantaleon Gonzales was going to leave his home. Gonzales lived on the western side of the Casita **volcano** in Nicaragua. It was not an **active** volcano. Even so, on October 30, 1998, Gonzales decided Casita was getting dangerous.

"It was raining very hard," said Gonzales. "I had this feeling that something terrible would happen. I could feel it in my bones. I was worried that the whole mountain would come down."

Rain, Rain, Rain

Gonzales had reason to worry. A **hurricane** called Mitch had moved close to Nicaragua and other countries in Central America. Like all hurricanes, Mitch had started off as a tropical storm. It began near the coast of Africa. As it moved west across the Atlantic Ocean, it gained strength. When its winds reached 74 miles per hour, Mitch was **labeled** a hurricane.

Soon Mitch had winds of 180 miles per hour. That made it one of the strongest hurricanes ever. As Mitch moved into the Caribbean Sea, its winds began to die down. So did its speed. On October 27, Mitch **stalled** off the coast of Central America. Day after day, it dumped rain on Nicaragua. Most of the time, rain is measured in inches. But the heavy rains from Hurricane Mitch were measured in feet! In some places more than two feet of rain fell.

As Pantaleon Gonzales watched the rain pouring down, he thought about the volcano towering above him. Casita had survived other storms. But this time Gonzales just wasn't sure the mountain would survive. He could not remember this much rain ever falling before.

As Gonzales feared, the rain was causing problems for the volcano. Casita had a **crater** at the top. This deep hole was being filled with rainwater. The water was putting pressure on the sides of the volcano. By the morning of October 30, the pressure was quite **intense**. The sides of the volcano were about ready to burst open.

A Family Survives

At the time, no one knew that the volcano was gettng close to its breaking point. But Gonzales trusted his **instinct**. He had a feeling everyone on the mountain was in danger. That morning he gathered his wife and six children. He told them they had to **vacate** their home. At 11:30 A.M. they got ready to leave their home and the village.

Hurricane Mitch stalled off the coast of Central America.

The volcano's crater filled with rainwater.

Half an hour later, Casita split open. The western side of the volcano's wall gave way. Water from inside the crater began streaming out. It was like water being poured from a pitcher. The water quickly flooded the hillside. As the water mixed with dirt, it formed thick heavy mud.

This river of mud ripped up everything it hit. The mudslide carried away trees, houses, animals, and people. It peeled away a strip of earth 300 feet wide and 60 feet deep. The mudslide flowed six miles to the bottom of the mountain. It kept going another eight miles until it reached the Pacific Ocean. By then, it had wiped out four villages. Most of the houses in these villages were buried under six feet of mud. So were most of the people.

Pantaleon Gonzales and his family got off Casita just in time. As they left their village, the water was already up to their waists. "I left with my wife and my children and hardly anything else," he said. They walked away as fast as they could. Soon after they left, the mudslide swept over their home and the entire village. "There's nothing left," Gonzales later said. "I've lost everything. But at least we're still alive. My friends, they're all dead."

Heavy mud flowed through the villages.

Life After Mitch

Before the mudslide, there had been 2,000 people living in villages on the western side of Casita. Fewer than 200 of them survived. Many of the survivors were badly hurt. They huddled together in the few houses that remained. "Everyone had broken bones, scratches, deep cuts," said survivor Mariana Centeno. People had to wait two days for the mud to harden. Only then could they begin to move around again.

In time, Hurricane Mitch and its rains died out. But by then, the storm had taken the lives of 10,000 Central American people. It was one of the worst **natural disasters** ever.

A few weeks after the mudslide, Pantaleon Gonzales walked back up the mountain. He wanted to see what was left of his village. One look was more than enough. "I won't ever go back there again," Gonzales said. "It hurts too much."

Others hoped to rebuild their homes and villages. They knew it would take months or even years. They hoped they could someday return to live on the western side of the Casita volcano.

Read and Remember — Finish the Sentence

Circle the best ending for each sentence.

1. Pantaleon Gonzales lived in _____ .

Africa   Nicaragua   the United States

2. Hurricanes begin as _____ .

snowstorms   earthquakes   tropical storms

3. Pantaleon Gonzales decided to _____ .

climb up Casita   leave the mountain   stay in his home

4. When Pantaleon Gonzales packed up his family, the neighbors _____ .

cried   laughed   watched

5. Four villages were destroyed by a _____ .

river of mud   strong wind   huge ocean wave

6. Survivors could not move around until the _____ .

mud hardened   smoke cleared   wind died down

Think About It — Find the Main Ideas

Underline the two most important ideas from the story.

1. A mudslide killed nearly 2,000 people.

2. Most of the time, rain is measured in inches.

3. Pantaleon Gonzales had six children.

4. Hurricane Mitch hit during the month of October.

5. Casita stood near the Pacific Ocean.

6. The rains from Hurricane Mitch caused Casita to split open.

Focus on Vocabulary — Find the Meaning

Read each sentence. Circle the best meaning for the word in dark print.

1. Casita was the name of a **volcano**.

   mountain with hot gas　　　huge rock　　　strong storm

2. It was not an **active** volcano.

   very strong　　　very big　　　ready to explode

3. A **hurricane** moved across the Atlantic Ocean.

   strong storm　　　large ship　　　small wave

4. Mitch was **labeled** a hurricane.

   named　　　moved by　　　ended by

5. The storm **stalled** off the coast of Central America.

   began　　　was noticed　　　stopped moving

6. There was a **crater** on top.

   pile of rocks　　　big hole　　　wooden house

7. The pressure was **intense**.

   very strong　　　only on the inside　　　hard to explain

8. Gonzales trusted his **instinct**.

   family　　　feelings　　　neighbors

9. He said they had to **vacate** their home.

   fix up　　　leave　　　share

10. It was one of the worst **natural disasters** ever.

    terrible events in nature　　　new ideas　　　places to live

Hurricanes

Hurricanes are powerful storms with strong winds and **rainstorms**. Hurricanes begin over warm ocean waters. They weaken after moving over land areas. The map below shows the areas in which most hurricanes occur. Study the map. Write the answer to each question.

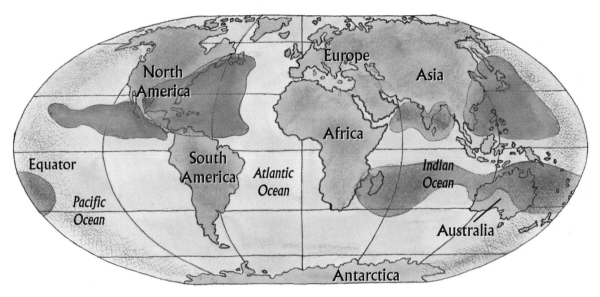

Average number of hurricanes per year	
More than 5	Less than 5

1. What color shows that an area gets less than five hurricanes a year? _____

2. Does Australia get more than five hurricanes a year? _____
   _____

3. How many hurricanes occur in the Indian Ocean? _____
   _____

4. What is a hurricane? _____
   _____

5. Where do hurricanes begin? _____

Caught by Surprise

Sarah Finch and Steven Newton both loved climbing mountains. They didn't know much about winter climbing. They wanted to learn about climbing in ice and snow. So Finch and Newton signed up for a winter skills class with a **guide** named Roger Wild. Four of their friends also signed up. On December 29, 1998, the group began the two-day class on Aonach Mor, a mountain in Scotland.

One of the things Wild taught was how to look out for avalanches. An avalanche can hit when no one expects it. Even an expert guide like Wild can be caught by surprise.

No Time to Run

Aonach Mor is not much more than a big hill. It has an **elevation** of only 4,000 feet. Still, it gets lots of snow and ice during the winter. Also, the mountain is quite steep. So avalanches can occur.

On the first day, Wild gathered Finch, Newton, and the others near the top of the mountain. He gave them ice axes. He also gave them helmets and special shoes for climbing on ice. Then they headed toward an icy area to try out their **equipment**.

Wild **estimated** it would take 45 minutes to get to the icy area. But the wind was blowing hard. It took them over an hour. When they got there, Wild asked everyone to put on the helmets. He told them to put their backpacks on the ground and wait a minute. He wanted to make sure the ice was safe for climbing.

Wild turned around and took a few steps away from everyone. Then suddenly he was buried by a huge wave of snow. Everyone else was buried, too. The avalanche of snow had hit the class members

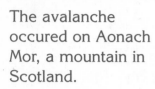

The avalanche occured on Aonach Mor, a mountain in Scotland.

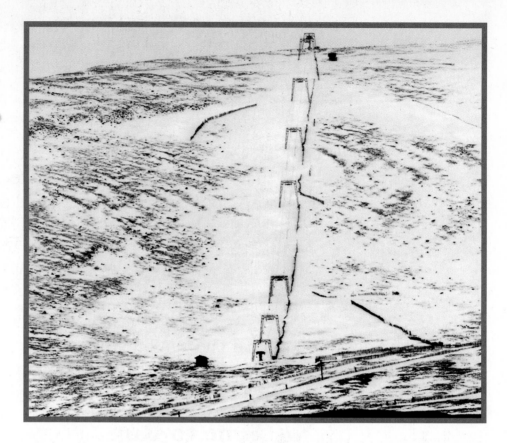

from behind. It had come crashing down from above. No one had been looking up, so no one had seen the avalanche coming.

"It just came toward us," said Newton. "But we couldn't move. We didn't have time to get out of the way."

"It just knocked us off our feet," added Finch. "I think I tried to stand up, but couldn't."

Getting Some Air

Finch, Newton, and Wild were the only ones who lived through the avalanche. They were alive, but trapped under the snow. Luckily, most of the snow was soft. They were able to push it around and open up small air pockets. Finch did that by moving her hand in front of her face.

Newton had been knocked out when the snow hit him. But when he awoke, he began to shake his head wildly. He, too, cleared just enough room to breathe.

The avalanche occurred at 10:30 A.M. But no one else knew about it. At 9:30 P.M. Wild's wife reported him missing. Only then did a rescue team head for the mountain.

By then, Steve Newton had managed to poke his hand up out of the snow. An ice axe had been buried right on top of him. He used it to cut a hole up through the **surface**. Newton could stick one hand out and then the other, but he couldn't get out the rest of his body. His legs remained firmly **wedged** under the snow. "I couldn't get my feet loose at all," he said.

From time to time, Finch, Newton, and Wild screamed for help. But **sound waves** do not travel well through snow. It was like screaming into a pillow. The snow **absorbed** all the sound. Sarah Finch screamed for hours and no one heard her. Newton and Wild also shouted as loud as they could. But the shouting did no good.

Climbing snowy mountains can be dangerous.

Screams in the Night

As the hours dragged by, Newton kept trying to dig out of the hole in the snow. He hoped rescuers would see where he was buried. At 1:30 the next morning, the rescuers got to the area. They saw Newton. Quickly they pulled Newton out and began to dig for the others.

As rescuers dug toward Finch, she kept up her screaming. "I was shouting all night," she said. But she was buried so deep the rescuers couldn't hear her. "Even when they were digging me out, they couldn't hear me shouting," she said.

At last, the three survivors were all safely out of the snow. They had been buried alive for 16 hours. Yet none of them was badly hurt. They just had a few bumps and bruises. Still, they would never forget the **terror** of their hours under the snow. Someone asked Newton if he still wanted to do winter climbing. "Not for a while," he answered. "It will take quite a while to **come to terms** with what has happened, the loss of our good friends." For the moment," he added, "we just want to get home."

Newton and Finch were glad to be alive and safe.

Read and Remember — Choose the Answer

Draw a circle around the correct answer.

1. What did Finch and Newton want to learn about?

   skiing   winter climbing   running races

2. What did Wild ask everyone to wear?

   snowshoes   helmets   sunglasses

3. What did Sarah Finch do while she was trapped?

   cried   shouted   slept

4. How long were Finch, Wild, and Newton buried?

   nine hours   sixteen hours   twenty-four hours

5. What were Finch and Newton buried under?

   mud   snow   rocks

Write About It

Imagine you are Sarah Finch or Steve Newton. Write a short letter to a friend, describing what happened to you.

Dear _____,

_____

_____

_____

_____

_____

_____

_____

Focus on Vocabulary — Match Up

Match each word with its meaning. Darken the circle beside the correct answer.

1. guide

⃝ friend   ⃝ leader   ⃝ player

2. elevation

⃝ height   ⃝ machine   ⃝ set of stairs

3. equipment

⃝ place to live   ⃝ fight   ⃝ tools

4. estimated

⃝ made a good guess   ⃝ ran quickly   ⃝ became upset

5. surface

⃝ the top layer   ⃝ a clean space   ⃝ wet feet

6. wedged

⃝ scraped   ⃝ stuck   ⃝ lost color

7. sound waves

⃝ silent winds   ⃝ bursts of water   ⃝ how sound travels

8. absorbed

⃝ fell slowly   ⃝ took in   ⃝ cut into small pieces

9. terror

⃝ speed   ⃝ memories   ⃝ great fear

10. come to terms

⃝ pay   ⃝ accept   ⃝ arrive

Avalanche Slopes

A **slab avalanche** is a large block of solid snow crumbling down a mountain. The **angle** of a mountain **slope** affects whether a slab avalanche occurs. The angle is measured in **degrees**. Use the diagrams below to compare mountain slopes. Circle the answer to each question.

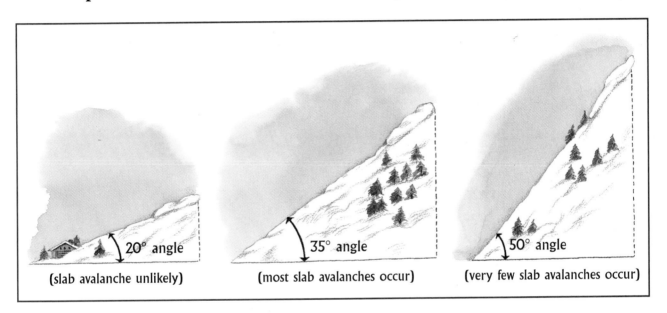

20° angle	35° angle	50° angle
(slab avalanche unlikely)	(most slab avalanches occur)	(very few slab avalanches occur)

1. Which of these slope angles is the steepest?

   20 degrees   35 degrees   50 degrees

2. On what angle slope is a slab avalanche most likely to occur?

   20 degrees   35 degrees   50 degrees

3. Which slope angle is the least steep?

   20 degrees   35 degrees   50 degrees

4. What affects whether a slab avalanche will occur?

   heavy snowfall   angle of mountain slope   top of mountain

5. What kind of snow is in a slab avalanche?

   wet snow   dry snow   solid snow

A New Year's Party Turns Deadly

At exactly midnight guns were fired to mark the start of 1999. People hugged and kissed each other. Some offered special wishes for a better year. The shouts of "Happy New Year!" were in the air.

By 1:30 A.M. hundreds of people had gathered in the school gym of a tiny town in northern Quebec, Canada. About 600 Inuit people lived in this tiny town. Over 400 of them were in the gym. They didn't know the school was about to be destroyed.

A Strange Noise

The party went on and on. There was plenty of meat, fish, and cake to eat. The adults danced to loud music. The children played games. Then, just before 2 A.M., disaster struck.

A massive wall of snow roared down a 500-foot hill behind the school. People later remembered a strange noise. "It was like an **explosion**," said Jean Leduc, the school's principal. Said Mayor Maggie Emudluk, "It sounded like thunder but only for a few seconds."

The force of the avalanche was amazing. It swept up trucks and **snowmobiles** that lay in its path. The rushing snow picked up a 31-year-old man. He had been standing outside the gym. The snow hit him so hard that he was driven right through the wall of the school. He suffered a broken **spine** but somehow survived.

When the avalanche of snow hit the school, one side of the building caved in. Tons and tons of snow spilled into the classrooms. School principal Jean Leduc later said the classrooms were "full of snow

The avalanche forced a snowmobile through the gym's wall.

like a bag of flour." The snow also crashed into the gym, burying many of the people there.

"The wall was flying into pieces," said Leduc. "The next thing you knew, the gym was entirely covered in snow."

Digging Out

Six people died instantly. Others were trapped under as much as ten feet of snow. People began to cry and scream. Leduc said there were "a few seconds of panic. After that people started to get a grip on themselves."

Those who were not buried knew what they had to do. They had to start digging right away. Many of their friends, neighbors, and family members were buried under the snow. These people might still be alive. But they wouldn't last long.

Mary Baron had been sitting in the gym when the avalanche hit. Her three-year-old son, Matthew, had been sitting next to her. "I wasn't buried completely," Baron said. But her son was. Quickly she started to dig for him.

Freezing cold air **swirled** into the gym. Outside the temperature was below zero. Soon the temperature inside wasn't much warmer. **Gusts** of wind whipped through the gym at 60 miles per hour.

The survivors didn't let that stop them. "People were looking for their kids, their husbands, wives, and parents," said Leduc. They used whatever they could find as tools. Only a few had shovels. Most dug with their bare hands. "I was digging with a frying pan," said teacher Anne Lanteigne.

Hard Questions

No outside help came to the village for nine hours. But that was not surprising. The villagers lived so far north that they often had to **rely** on themselves. The nearest police station, for example, was 190 miles away. On this night, snow and blowing wind kept rescuers away. It was morning before doctors and nurses could get there.

The gym was full of snow.

As the sun rose, people could see just how much damage had been done. The school was destroyed. Trucks and snowmobiles had been shoved through walls. Drawings made by children lay **crumpled** in the snow.

Worse, nine people had died. Five of them were children under the age of eight. Twenty-five others were **injured**. Twelve of them had to be taken to a hospital in Montreal, one thousand miles away.

The survivors were badly shaken by what had happened. They wanted to know what had caused the avalanche. But no one was sure. The guns that were fired at midnight might have done it. The **vibrations** from these gunshots could have **jarred** the snow loose. The loud music could have done it, too. Or perhaps the avalanche was not caused by people at all. Perhaps it was just a case of nature showing how powerful it really is.

People do not know what caused the terrible avalanche.

Read and Remember — Finish the Sentence

Circle the best ending for each sentence.

1. A New Year's party was held at the _____.
   school   hospital   police station

2. One of the people at the party was _____.
   a policeman   a principal   a pilot

3. At midnight some people _____.
   rode a snowmobile   climbed a mountain   fired guns

4. The school was in front of a _____.
   hill   lake   group of stores

5. To dig through the snow, most people used _____.
   snow plows   ice axes   bare hands

6. The air in the gym became very _____.
   smoky   thick   cold

Think About It — Find the Sequence

Number the sentences to show the correct order from the story. The first one is done for you.

_____ **1.** People heard a noise that sounded like thunder.

_____ **2.** Doctors and nurses arrived at the scene.

_____ **3.** Anne Lanteigne dug through the snow with a frying pan.

_____ **4.** The rushing snow drove a man right through a wall.

___1___ **5.** People shouted "Happy New Year!"

_____ **6.** Twelve people were treated at a hospital in Montreal.

Focus on Vocabulary — Make a Word

Choose a word in dark print to complete each sentence. Write the letters of the word on the blanks. When you are finished, the letters in the circles will tell what was happening in the gym before the avalanche hit.

jarred   **explosion**   **crumpled**   **spine**   **rely**

swirled   **vibrations**   **snowmobiles**   **injured**   **gusts**

1. The heavy snow was _____ loose.
   ◯ _ _ _ _

2. The avalanche sounded like an _____.
   ◯ _ _ _ _ _ _ _ _

3. The avalanche swept up _____.
   ◯ _ _ _ _ _ _ _ _ _ _

4. Drawings lay _____ in the snow.
   ◯ _ _ _ _ _ _ _

5. Freezing cold air _____ into the gym.
   _ _ _ _ _ ◯ _

6. One man had a broken _____.
   ◯ _ _ _ _

7. The avalanche may have been caused by _____.
   _ _ _ ◯ _ _ _

8. Twenty-five people were _____.
   _ _ _ ◯ _ _ _

9. Strong _____ of wind whipped through the gym.
   _ _ ◯ _ _

10. The villagers often had to _____ on themselves.
    _ _ ◯ _

Avalanche Conditions

Certain conditions affect whether an **avalanche** will start. The chart below describes conditions that are present in the beginning of an avalanche. Study the chart. Write the answer to each question.

Avalanche Conditions		
Weather	wind speed and direction →	Mountain slopes that do not get direct wind are more likely to have avalanches.
	temperature →	Warmer temperatures can increase the chance of an avalanche.
Ground	mountain slope angle →	Most slab avalanches occur on slopes with an angle of 30–45 degrees.
	surface →	Smooth areas have an increased chance for avalanches.
	plant life →	Avalanches rarely begin in areas with many trees.
Snow	fresh snowfall →	Heavy, fresh snowfall greatly increases the chance for an avalanche.
	large amounts of snow build up during one time period →	When the total amount of snow buildup cracks easily, an avalanche can occur.

1. What are the three main conditions that show whether an avalanche can occur? _____

_____

2. What temperatures increase the chance for an avalanche?

_____

3. How do plants affect whether an avalanche will occur?

_____

4. On what kind of mountain slope do slab avalanches occur most?

_____

5. What ground surface has an increased chance for avalanches?

_____

Survivors in the Rubble

It was just past three in the morning on August 17, 1999. Most people living in **northwestern** Turkey were fast asleep. Suddenly an earthquake rocked the entire area.

The earthquake measured 7.4 on the Richter scale. That made it one of the most powerful earthquakes ever. It killed 15,000 people. It left 600,000 others without homes. The tragedy saddened the world. Yet even in the middle of disaster, some amazing stories of **survival** came through.

97 Hours

Yuksel Er was one who survived. He had been having trouble sleeping that night. So he was moving around his third-floor apartment when the earthquake hit. All six stories of his apartment building collapsed around him. "It was awful," he said. As he fell through space, he felt like he was "in a **whirlwind**." Seconds later, Er found himself lying on his back in total darkness. Rubble was all around him. A heavy door lay just inches from his chest and stomach.

At first Er thought the world had ended. Later, he realized what had happened. Hoping someone would find him, he whistled loudly. He banged on a wall near his head. But no one heard him. As the hours passed, Er became quiet. He knew he had to save his strength. That was the only way to stay alive.

Hour after hour Er lay trapped in a space no bigger than the size of a coffin or small bed. He could not roll over nor could he sit up. Er grew hungry. Even more than that, he grew thirsty. He would have given anything for a drop of water. He also suffered from the heat. "Where I was lying got extremely hot at **midday**," Er said. It was "almost like a fire was lit underneath me."

Er tried to cheer himself by thinking of family and friends. But one memory made him sad. The night before the earthquake, he had spoken angrily to his 13-year-old son, Eser. He was mad because the boy had been using the family computer for six straight hours. Now Er wondered if he would ever see Eser again.

Finally on the fourth day, rescuers found Yuksel Er. By then he was **exhausted** and quite weak. Yet as rescuers helped him out, he managed to stand up. As he did, people cheered. Best of all, his son Eser was alive and well and waiting for him.

133 Hours

Yuksel Er had lasted 97 hours in the rubble. Experts say that is about as long as people can hold out. After that, they die from **dehydration**, which means lack of water. But 18-year-old Dilek Aslan lasted even longer. She was found alive after 133 hours.

The powerful earthquake caused many buildings in Turkey to collapse.

Rescue workers help a survivor out of the rubble.

Aslan was in her bed when the earthquake hit. As the ground shook, her 11-story apartment building collapsed. Aslan was caught under tons of steel and cement. She wasn't hurt, but she was trapped in a very small space. She couldn't stand up or lie down. She could only **crouch** in the dark and hope to be found.

"For the first two days, all I did was cry," she said. "I cried and cried." After that, she drifted in and out of sleep. At times, she dreamed she had been rescued. She imagined she was talking happily with friends. Other times, her mind cleared and she saw that she was still trapped in the wreckage. At last, on the sixth day, rescuers reached Aslan. They pulled her out and set her safely in her father's arms.

146 Hours

Of all the people buried in the earthquake, none lasted longer than little Ismail Cimen. This four-year-old boy survived an amazing 146 hours under the rubble. Ismail's father and three of his sisters were killed in the earthquake. His mother, Serife, was badly hurt. But rescuers were able to get to Serife quickly. She was rushed to the hospital right away. Serife was **heartbroken** to learn that so many of her family members had died. She could not believe what had happened. Serife wished to have her family back. "I went crazy," she said.

In fact, Ismail was still alive. When his apartment building fell, he became wedged under a collapsed **balcony**. There he stayed for six full days. He crouched there, all alone, in the dark. He had nothing to eat. He had nothing to drink. His lips became dry and cracked. Dehydration made him weaker and weaker. A rash broke out on his chest. He lost eleven pounds.

Finally, rescuers pulled the wreckage away from him. They rushed him to the hospital. When Serife heard that Ismail was alive, she was **overcome** with happiness. She said she "went crazy again, but this time with joy."

Four-year-old Ismail Cimen was found alive after six days.

Read and Remember — Check the Events

Place a check in front of the three sentences that tell what happened in the story.

_____ **1.** A deadly earthquake struck Turkey.

_____ **2.** Yuksel Er was trapped when his apartment collapsed.

_____ **3.** Dilek Aslan saved eighteen people all by herself.

_____ **4.** Rescue workers did not dare touch Dilek Aslan.

_____ **5.** Ismail Cimen survived 146 hours under the rubble.

_____ **6.** Serife Ismail climbed out a window to safety.

Write About It

Imagine you are one of the survivors in the story. Write a short paragraph describing how it felt to be trapped in the rubble and then rescued.

Focus on Vocabulary — Finish Up

Choose the correct word in dark print to complete each sentence.

exhausted	**northwestern**	**heartbroken**	**survival**
midday	**whirlwind**	**dehydration**	**overcome**
balcony	**crouch**		

1. To bend low is to _____.

2. The middle part of the day is called _____.

3. To be completely tired out is to be _____.

4. A _____ is air that is swirling around very fast.

5. When your feelings take over something, you are _____ by it.

6. A lack of water is called _____.

7. The direction that takes you to the north and west is called _____.

8. A small porch sticking out from the side of a building is a _____.

9. Living through a disaster is _____.

10. To be filled with great sadness is to be _____.

Richter Scale

Scientists study the strength of an **earthquake** using a **seismograph**. The results are given on the **Richter scale**. Study the information below. Circle the answer to each question.

Richter Scale		
	3	Dishes rattle.
	4	Many people can feel the earthquake. Walls become cracked.
	5	Earthquake feels strong. Weaker buildings are damaged.
1994, Los Angeles (6.7)	**6**	Most regular buildings are very damaged.
1989, San Francisco (7.1) 1999, Turkey (7.4)	**7**	Even strong buildings are destroyed.
1985, Mexico (8.1) 1933, Japan (8.5)	**8**	Buildings designed to survive earthquakes become very damaged.
1960, Chile (9.5)	**9**	Great damage and terrible loss of life occur all over the area.

1. What are damaged during an earthquake that registers 4.0 on the Richter scale?

weaker buildings   walls   stronger buildings

2. What strength earthquake can damage buildings designed to survive earthquakes?

3.0   6.0   8.0

3. What was the strength of the 1985 earthquake in Mexico?

8.1   6.7   4.2

4. Which earthquake was the most powerful?

1960, Chile   1933, Japan   1999, Turkey

5. What was the strength of the 1999 earthquake in Turkey?

7.1   7.4   8.5

GLOSSARY

▲ Words with this symbol can be found in the SCIENCE CONNECTION.

absorbed page 81
Absorbed means took in or sucked in.

acres page 49
Acres are units for measuring land. An acre equals 43,560 square feet.

active page 71
Active means being able or likely to explode.

air mass page 21
▲ An air mass is a large body of air.

amazingly page 66
Amazingly means surprisingly.

angle page 85
▲ An angle is the space between two straight lines that meet at a certain point. The space of an angle is measured in degrees.

assumed page 40
Assumed means to take for granted or to suppose that something is true.

avalanche pages 8, 85, 93
▲ An avalanche is a huge wall of snow sliding at fast speed down a mountain.

balcony page 98
A balcony is like a porch with a railing built out from the side of a building.

bruise page 33
A bruise is an injury that causes skin to turn colors, such as blue or purple.

cement page 17
Cement is a building material made from powdered clay and limestone mixed with water.

coast page 63
A coast is the shore of land along a sea or ocean.

collapsed page 24
Collapsed means fell down.

come to terms page 82
Come to terms means to get used to or learn to accept something that has happened.

community page 25
A community is a group of people living in the same area.

concrete page 55
Concrete is a mixture of cement, sand, and water. It is a strong building material.

confusion page 32
Confusion means not being sure of what is going on.

crater page 72
A crater is a deep hole in the ground or in a volcano.

credit page 66
Credit means thanks or praise.

crouch page 97
Crouch means to bend low or stoop over.

crumpled page 90
Crumpled means bent out of shape.

crust   pages 13, 29
The crust is Earth's rocky outer layer.

damaged   page 48
Damaged means harmed or ruined.

dazed   page 42
Dazed means not aware of things.

deafening   page 32
Deafening means loud enough to hurt the ears.

death toll   page 10
A death toll is the number of people who died during an event, such as a flood.

debris   page 41
Debris is broken pieces of material that are left after something is destroyed or broken down.

definitely   page 34
Definitely means without a doubt.

degrees   page 85
Degrees are units of measure for temperature, distance, and angle.

dehydration   page 96
Dehydration means a lack of water.

desperately   page 26
To do something desperately means to try very hard even though there is little hope of success.

destroyed   page 10
Destroyed means ruined or smashed.

detected   page 57
Detected means found where something is located.

disaster   page 7
A disaster is an event that happens suddenly and causes a lot of damage.

earthquake   pages 23, 29, 101
An earthquake is movement or shaking of Earth's crust.

elevation   page 79
Elevation is height above a given level, such as sea level.

equipment   page 79
Equipment is tools needed for a purpose, such as mountain climbing or playing sports.

erosion   pages 40, 45
Erosion is when wind, water, or some other process wears away the surface of Earth or other materials.

estimated   page 79
Estimated means made a good guess.

evergreen   page 31
An evergreen tree has leaves that stay green all year around.

exhausted   page 96
Exhausted means very tired.

explosion   page 87
An explosion is the act of blowing up.

fault   page 29
A fault is another name for a long crack in the ground.

forest rangers   page 31
Forest rangers are people who help protect forests.

frantically   page 66
Frantically means acting out of control or wildly.

front   pages 15, 21
A front is where one type of weather begins and another ends.

frost wedging   page 53
Frost wedging is a process that causes rocks to crack and break off from a cliff.

glacier   page 7
A glacier is a large sheet of ice and snow that moves very slowly.

granite   page 47
Granite is a very hard kind of rock.

gravity   page 61
The force that pulls objects toward Earth.

guide   page 79
A guide is a person who leads, teaches, or shows the way.

gushed   page 63
Gushed means a great amount of water or other liquid flowed very quickly.

gusts   page 89
Gusts are sudden strong bursts of wind.

heartbroken   page 98
Heartbroken means feeling very sad.

hillside   page 15
A hillside is one side of a hill.

hollowed   page 31
Hollowed means made a hole in something.

huddled   page 39
Huddled means crowded together.

hurricane   pages 71, 77
A hurricane is a storm that has very strong winds and usually occurs with rain, thunder, and lightning.

hypothermia   page 57
Hypothermia is when a person's body temperature is very low. People in very cold air or water can be in danger of hypothermia.

ice caves   page 31
Ice caves are holes formed in deep snow.

injured   page 90
Injured means wounded or hurt.

injuries   page 48
Injuries are places on a person's body that are hurt or wounded.

instinct   page 72
Instinct is feelings or talents that people are born with rather than those that are learned.

intense   page 72
Intense means very great or strong.

jarred   page 90
Jarred means shook or jolted.

labeled   page 71
Labeled means named or called.

landslide   page 55
A landslide is a large amount of earth and rock that slides down a steep hill or a mountain.

limestone   page 16
Limestone is rock that is mainly formed from shells and coral.

lodge   page 55
A lodge or an inn is a place to stay overnight.

lookout   page 50
Lookout means a careful watching or looking for something.

map key   page 69
A map key explains what the symbols or colors on a map mean.

massive   page 8
Massive means very large or heavy.

midday   page 96
Midday means the middle of the day or around noon.

mudslide   pages 17, 45
A mudslide is soft wet earth that moves down the side of a hill or a mountain.

natural disasters   page 74
Natural disasters are terrible events caused by nature, such as hurricanes or floods.

northwestern   page 95
Northwestern is a direction meaning in the north and west part of a place.

official   page 25
Official means in charge.

operated   page 49
Operated means gave medical treatment called surgery.

organized   page 24
Getting organized means forming a plan so that a group can work together.

orphanages   page 42
Orphanages are homes set up to care for children whose parents have died.

overcome   page 98
Overcome means to make helpless or to be taken over by strong emotional feelings.

panic   page 34
Panic is to have a sudden and very powerful feeling of fear.

pressure   page 50
Pressure is putting strain or stress on something.

rainstorm   pages 63, 77
A rainstorm is a storm with lots of rain.

rely   page 89
Rely means to count on or depend on.

rescuers   page 48
Rescuers are people who help others who are hurt or are in dangerous places.

result   page 42
A result is what comes about because something else happened. For example, the result of too much rain is a flood.

Richter scale   pages 23, 101
The Richter scale is a scale used to measure how strong an earthquake is.

rickety   page 41
Rickety means shaky or likely to fall apart.

risky   page 15

Risky means possibly dangerous.

riverbed   page 39

A riverbed is the ground over which a river flows or used to flow.

rockfalls   page 50

Rockfalls are when rocks suddenly fall from a cliff.

rubble   page 49

Rubble is a large bunch of rough or broken things, such as rocks.

scooped   page 63

Scooped means picked up.

seeped   page 7

Seeped means ran or flowed slowly.

seismograph   page 101

A seismograph is an instrument used by scientists to study the strength of an earthquake.

shattered   page 55

When something is shattered, it is ruined or broken into many pieces.

shield   page 63

Shield means to cover up or protect.

slab avalanche   page 85

A slab avalanche is a type of avalanche that has a large block of solid snow that moves down a mountain slope.

slabs   page 55

Slabs are large flat pieces of certain materials, such as concrete or stone.

slope   pages 8, 85

A slope is ground that slants downward or upward.

snowmobiles   page 87

Snowmobiles are sled-like machines with motors. They are made to travel over snow.

sound waves   page 81

Sound waves are waves of sound pressed through air or some other material. A sound wave cannot always be heard.

spine   page 87

The spine is the backbone or the bones down the back of a body.

squinting   page 65

Squinting means almost closing one's eyes to try to see better.

stable   page 15

Stable means fixed in place or not likely to move.

stalled   page 71

Stalled means stopped or quit moving forward.

suffered   page 42

Suffered means put up with or felt pain.

surface   page 81

A surface is the top layer or the outside of something.

survival   page 95

Survival means living through an event.

survived   page 10

Survived means stayed alive.

survivor   page 9

A survivor is a person who stays alive through a disaster, such as a flood or an avalanche.

swirled   page 89
Swirled means moved in circles.

temperature   pages 21, 57
Temperature is how hot or cold something is. Body temperature is measured in degrees by a thermometer.

terrified   page 63
Terrified means very scared.

terror   page 82
Terror means great fear.

tons   page 32
Tons are units of weight. One ton is 2,000 pounds.

total   page 56
Total means complete or perfect.

tragedy   page 18
A tragedy is a very unhappy or terrible event.

tropical storm   page 15
A tropical storm is a storm with very high winds and a great deal of rain.

underground spring   page 55
An underground spring is water that runs under the surface of the ground.

unit   page 25
A unit is a group of people that works together to get something done.

utility   page 16
A utility is something designed to be useful. For example, a utility pole is useful for holding up electric or telephone wires.

vacate   page 72
To vacate means to leave or get out of something.

vibrations   page 90
Vibrations are quick back and forth or trembling motions.

volcano   page 71
A volcano is a mountain or a hole in Earth's crust that can explode with lava, gases, hot rocks, or ashes.

volunteers   page 26
Volunteers are people who offer to do something because they want to do it.

weather map   page 69
A weather map is created by scientists to show what kind of weather to expect in different areas.

wedged   page 81
Wedged means stuck or forced into a narrow space.

whirlwind   page 95
A whirlwind is a windstorm in which the air is moving very fast in circles.

wreckage   page 24
Wreckage is the broken parts and pieces that are left after something has been crashed or wrecked.

Did You Know?

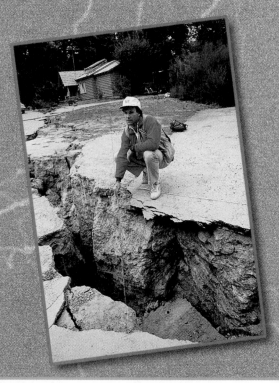

◀ Did you know that there are earthquakes happening every day? About once every 30 seconds the earth shakes somewhere in the world. Most of these earthquakes, however, are too small to do any damage.

Have you ever wondered how certain mountains are made? Some mountains are made when large pieces of Earth's crust hit each other or move apart. When this happens, part of Earth's inner layer rises to the surface and makes a mountain. ▶

◀ Have you ever wondered how long the longest earthquake lasted? The longest recorded earthquake was in Alaska. On March 27, 1964, people in Alaska felt the ground shake for four long minutes!

Have you ever wondered what ▶
causes mudslides? Mudslides
occur when too much water
from heavy rainfall or rapid snow
melting flows into the ground.
When the ground has too much
water, it can turn into a flowing
river of mud. The river of mud is
very powerful. It grows in size
and speed as it moves down a
mountain or hill!

◀ Do you know what
causes a sinkhole?
Underground water
slowly eats away hard
rock. Then a hole or
cave replaces the
rock. When the land
over the hole grows
too weak, it sinks.

How fast does an avalanche ▶
travel? Its speed depends on
its size. The range of speed
for an average avalanche is
56 to 168 miles per hour. The
fastest speed recorded for an
avalanche was about 280
miles per hour!

CHART YOUR SCORES

Score Your Work

1. Count the number of correct answers you have for each activity.
2. Write these numbers in the boxes in the chart.
3. Give yourself a score (maximum of 5 points) for **Write About It**.
4. Add up the numbers to get a final score for each tale.
5. Write your final score in the score box.
6. Compare your final score with the maximum score given for each story.

Tales	Read and Remember	Think About It	Write About It	Focus on Vocabulary	Science Connection	Score
Danger from Above						/23
A Dangerous Hill						/23
California Earthquake						/25
Trouble at Big Four Mountain						/25
Mudslide in Haiti						/26
In the Wrong Place at the Wrong Time						/26
Buried Alive						/25
Pulled from the Mud						/23
The Mountain That Washed Away						/23
Caught by Surprise						/25
A New Year's Party Turns Deadly						/27
Survivors in the Rubble						/23

Danger from Above Pages 6–13
Read and Remember — Choose the Answer:
1. talking a walk 2. Mt. Huascarán 3. a cloud
4. a terrible roar 5. a wall of mud 6. more than
3,500
Think About It — Find the Main Ideas: 3, 6
Focus on Vocabulary — Find the Meaning:
1. terrible event 2. sheet of ice 3. flowed slowly
4. very large 5. slanted ground 6. sliding snow
and mud 7. person who lived 8. stayed alive
9. completely ruined 10. number of people
who died
Science Connection — Forming Mountains:
1. crust 2. Land is pushed up along cracks
in the crust. 3. fold mountains 4. volcanic
mountains, dome mountains 5. block
mountains, volcanic mountains

A Dangerous Hill Pages 14–21
Read and Remember — Check the Events:
2, 4, 5
Write About It: Answers will vary.
Focus on Vocabulary — Make a Word:
1. tropical 2. mudslide 3. stable 4. risky
5. utility 6. limestone 7. tragedy 8. hillside
9. cement 10. front. The letters in the circles
spell *Puerto Rico*.
Science Connection — Fronts: 1. a large body
of air 2. a front 3. both 4. cold front 5. Warm
air rises above cold air.

California Earthquake Pages 22–29
Read and Remember — Finish the Sentence:
1. freeway 2. tools 3. cars 4. survivors
5. firefighters 6. caught
Think About It — Drawing Conclusions:
Answers will vary. Here are some possible
conclusions. 1. He was in a hurry to see what
damage had been done. 2. She wanted to get to
safety. 3. He thought these items could be used
to help get people off the freeway. 4. He thought
people could be saved if he organized a rescue.
Focus on Vocabulary — Finish the Paragraphs:
1. earthquake 2. Richter scale 3. collapsed
4. wreckage 5. desperately 6. organized
7. community 8. volunteers 9. unit 10. official

Science Connection — Earthquakes:
1. fault 2. focus 3. epicenter 4. Large pieces of
Earth's crust move suddenly. 5. shock waves

Trouble at Big Four Mountain
Pages 30–37
Read and Remember — Choose the Answer:
1. to look around 2. outside the cave 3. her
glasses 4. a camping knife 5. He hated small
spaces.
Write About It: Answers will vary.
Focus on Vocabulary — Match Up:
1. always has green leaves 2. big holes in snow
3. carved out 4. people who protect the forest
5. very loud 6. units of weight 7. not being sure
8. hurt skin that looks blue 9. feel very
frightened 10. without doubt
Science Connection — Mountain Plants:
1. timber line 2. alpine meadow 3. Air is cold
and thin. Wind is very strong. 4. evergreen trees
and leafy trees 5. no

Mudslide in Haiti Pages 38–45
Read and Remember — Check the Events:
2, 3, 4
Think About It — Fact or Opinion:
1. O 2. F 3. F 4. O 5. F 6. F 7. O 8. O
Focus on Vocabulary — Crossword Puzzle:
ACROSS — 1. result 5. orphanages 6. riverbed
9. dazed 10. suffered DOWN — 2. erosion
3. assumed 4. huddled 7. rickety 8. debris
Science Connection — Mudslides:
1. mudslides 2. most 3. a mudslide 4. floods
5. trees

In the Wrong Place at the Wrong Time
Pages 46–53
Read and Remember — Finish the Sentence:
1. have fun 2. large 3. cloud of dust 4. snack
bar 5. trees 6. seeing
Write About It: Answers will vary.
Focus on Vocabulary — Finish Up:
1. damaged 2. granite 3. operated 4. rescuers
5. pressure 6. rockfalls 7. injuries 8. rubble
9. acres 10. lookout

Science Connection — Rockfalls:
1. Rain seeps into cracks in rocks. 2. ice 3. It grows in size. 4. Water enters the cracks and freezes. 5. Park workers worry about rockfalls because they can cause harm to things and people.

Buried Alive Pages 54–61
Read and Remember — Choose the Answer:
1. Australia 2. in bed 3. water 4. cave darkness 5. He became cold.
Think About It — Cause and Effect:
1. e 2. b 3. d 4. a 5. c
Focus on Vocabulary — Finish the Paragraphs:
1. Lodge 2. shattered 3. landslide 4. slabs 5. concrete 6. underground spring 7. total 8. detected 9. temperature 10. hypothermia
Science Connection — Downhill Movement:
1. landslide, mudflow, slump 2. earthflow, creep 3. An earthflow is a slow downhill movement of soil and plants. 4. earthquake, volcano eruption, or heavy rain 5. creep

Pulled from the Mud Pages 62–69
Read and Remember — Check the Events:
1, 4, 5
Write About It: Answers will vary.
Focus on Vocabulary — Crossword Puzzle:
ACROSS — 2. rainstorm 5. terrified 7. frantically 8. scooped 9. gushed. DOWN — 1. coast 3. amazingly 4. squinting 6. credit 8. shield
Science Connection — Weather Map:
1. 2. yellow 3. rainy 4. Detroit 5. New York

The Mountain That Washed Away
Pages 70–77
Read and Remember — Finish the Sentence:
1. Nicaragua 2. tropical storms 3. leave the mountain 4. laughed 5. river of mud 6. mud hardened
Think About It — Find the Main Ideas: 1, 6
Focus on Vocabulary — Find the Meaning:
1. mountain with hot gas 2. ready to explode 3. strong storm 4. named 5. stopped moving 6. big hole 7. very strong 8. feelings 9. leave 10. terrible events in nature

Science Connection — Hurricanes: 1. blue 2. no 3. less than five 4. A hurricane is a powerful storm with strong winds and rainstorms. 5. Hurricanes begin over warm ocean waters.

Caught by Surprise Pages 78–85
Read and Remember — Choose the Answer:
1. winter climbing 2. helmets 3. shouted 4. sixteen hours 5. snow
Write About It: Answers will vary.
Focus on Vocabulary — Match Up:
1. leader 2. height 3. tools 4. made a good guess 5. the top layer 6. stuck 7. how sound travels 8. took in 9. great fear 10. accept
Science Connection — Avalanche Slopes:
1. 50 degrees 2. 35 degrees 3. 20 degrees 4. angle of mountain slope 5. solid snow

A New Year's Party Turns Deadly
Pages 86–93
Read and Remember — Finish the Sentence:
1. school 2. a principal 3. fired guns 4. hill 5. bare hands 6. cold
Think About It — Find the Sequence:
1. 2 2. 5 3. 4 4. 3 5. 1 6. 6
Focus on Vocabulary — Make a Word:
1. jarred 2. explosion 3. snowmobiles 4. crumpled 5. swirled 6. spine 7. vibrations 8. injured 9. gusts 10. rely. The letters in the circles spell *a loud party.*
Science Connection — Avalanche Conditions:
1. weather, ground, snow 2. warmer temperatures 3. Avalanches rarely begin in areas with many trees. 4. slopes with angles of 30–45 degrees 5. smooth areas

Survivors in the Rubble Pages 94–101
Read and Remember — Check the Events:
1, 2, 5
Write About It: Answers will vary.
Focus on Vocabulary — Finish Up:
1. crouch 2. midday 3. exhausted 4. whirlwind 5. overcome 6. dehydration 7. northwestern 8. balcony 9. survival 10. heartbroken
Science Connection — Richter Scale:
1. walls 2. 8.0 3. 8.1 4. 1960, Chile 5. 7.4